PRAISE FOR THE MEASURE OF A CHURCH

Sometimes it is difficult to know for sure if your church is really all that God wants it to be. *The Measure of a Church* will help you find the answer. Gene Getz has given us a remarkable, accurate guidebook for lifting our churches to a new level.

C. PETER WAGNER, CHANCELLOR
WAGNER LEADERSHIP INSTITUTE

Great communicators need a vision and they must be able to effectively deliver their message. In *The Measure of a Church*, Gene Getz has exceeded in not only painting a vivid picture of what a church can be, but also in backing up with indisputable scriptural moorings. He has identified the fundamental tenets we can all use to determine whether our churches are up to the expectations established by Paul and the disciples when they planted the first New Testament congregations. Successful leaders must have the courage to take action while others waiver. Do not hesitate to measure your church or to make the necessary improvements. The optimist expects change. A leader adjusts the sails. With this book, Getz unfolds a map that will enable us to chart a sound course for our churches and to shape congregations that truly reflect God's grace.

JOHN MAXWELL, FOUNDER
THE INJOY GROUP

The MEASURE *of a* CHURCH

GENE A. GETZ

From Gospel Light
Ventura, California, U.S.A.

Published by Regal Books
Gospel Light
Ventura, California, U.S.A.
Printed in the U.S.A.

Regal Books is a ministry of Gospel Light, an evangelical Christian publisher dedicated to serving the local church. We believe God's vision for Gospel Light is to provide church leaders with biblical, user-friendly materials that will help them evangelize, disciple and minister to children, youth and families.

It is our prayer that this Regal book will help you discover biblical truth for your own life and help you meet the needs of others. May God richly bless you.

For a free catalog of resources from Regal Books/Gospel Light, please call your Christian supplier or contact us at 1-800-4-GOSPEL *or* www.regalbooks.com.

All words emphasized by the author in Scripture quotes appear in italics.

Cover and Inside Design by Robert Williams
Edited by Steven Lawson

Library of Congress Cataloging-in-Publication Data
Getz, Gene A.
The measure of a church / by Gene A. Getz.
p. cm.
Includes bibliographical references.
ISBN 0-8307-2774-4
1. Church. 2. Love—Religious aspects—Christianity. 3. Hope—Religious aspects—Christianity. 4. Faith. I. Title.

BV600.3 .G48 2002
262—dc21 2001048862

1 2 3 4 5 6 7 8 9 10 11 12 13 14 15 / 09 08 07 06 05 04 03 02 01

Rights for publishing this book in other languages are contracted by Gospel Light Worldwide, the international nonprofit ministry of Gospel Light. Gospel Light Worldwide also provides publishing and technical assistance to international publishers dedicated to producing Sunday School and Vacation Bible School curricula and books in the languages of the world. For additional information, visit www.gospellightworldwide.org; write to Gospel Light Worldwide, P.O. Box 3875, Ventura, CA 93006; or send an e-mail to info@gospellightworldwide.org.

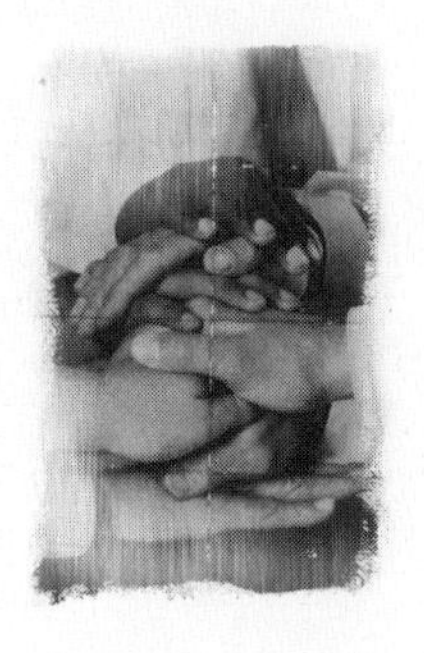

Dedication

I am dedicating this book to Dr. Howard Hendricks, who initially entrusted me with his department and classes at Dallas Theological Seminary while he was on sabbatical. With this assignment also came the freedom to address the challenges that faced the Church in the latter part of the twentieth century. Eventually this freedom led me out of the seminary classroom and into a church-planting ministry.

Thanks, Howie, for opening the door to an opportunity that has changed my life.

Contents

Foreword 9
A Ministry of Multiplication

Acknowledgments 11

Introduction 12
A Great Adventure

Chapter 1 17
God's Mystery Revealed

Chapter 2 35
Metaphors That Measure

Chapter 3 51
The Perfect Measurement

Chapter 4 72
Reflecting God's Grace

Chapter 5 96
A Divine Trilogy

Chapter 6 122
Faith That Works

Chapter 7 146
Hope That Endures

Chapter 8 169
Love—The Greatest of These

Chapter 9 194
Measuring Our Leaders

Chapter 10 211
Measuring Corporate Worship

Chapter 11 229
The Measure of a Church—Principles to Guide Us

Appendix A 245
Use of the Word "Church" (*Ekklesia*) in the Book of
Acts and the Epistles

Appendix B. 249
Descriptions of Local New Testament Churches

Appendix C 265
Paul's Journeys—A Time Line

Appendix D 266
Chronology of Paul's Life

FOREWORD

A MINISTRY OF MULTIPLICATION

One of the most significant decisions of my ministry was my invitation to Dr. Gene Getz to join our Christian Education Department at Dallas Seminary. Since it was a rapidly growing theological emphasis in the Church, we needed someone to enrich our seminary education with creativity and reliable biblical teaching. Gene made a profound contribution in both the classroom and in leadership responsibilities.

At that time Gene was forging the philosophy of ministry that he eventually used to launch the Fellowship Bible Church movement. His own study of the Word of God provided the seedbed, but it was my privilege to release him to begin the journey. On many occasions we discussed his thinking and rationale for how a church ought to operate. I encouraged him to go for it.

That Gene did! But, as always, it was not enough to come up with a set of theories. Those ideas needed to be tested in the laboratory of life. So Gene became involved in founding the first Fellowship Bible Church in Dallas, Texas. Its impact was profound, not only in our city but also across the country as his concepts were put into practice in the ministry of graduating students and other individuals in local church ministries. Now all over the United States and around the world churches exist as products of this vision.

I personally believe that Gene's efforts represent one of the great contributions to the Body of Christ. Gene's work has greatly enriched the city of Dallas—nearly 30,000 people in the area worship at Fellowship Bible Churches. As I travel, even internationally, I have discovered that seeds planted by Gene Getz have flowered into churches that the hand of God is upon in this generation.

The book you are about to read has grown out of Gene Getz's total experiences, first as my associate at Dallas Seminary and then as a church-planting pioneer. These pages have been renewed and updated since the publication of his previous book by the same title, bringing fresh insights from Gene's continuing study of the New Testament. Read carefully! This book could change your total perspective on how to measure success in the local church.

Howard G. Hendricks
Distinguished Professor and Chairman
Center for Christian Leadership
Dallas Theological Seminary

ACKNOWLEDGMENTS

I wish to express deep appreciation to my fellow elders, pastors and staff at Fellowship Bible Church North who have served with me so faithfully in the ministry. It is a great privilege to join hands and hearts with men and women who are consistently committed to becoming "mature, attaining to the whole measure of the fullness of Christ" (Eph. 4:13).

INTRODUCTION

A GREAT ADVENTURE

A few years ago, I noticed something that really grabbed my attention. It was one of those *aha!* moments in life. I was exploring the New Testament to see what God intends the Church to be. I was a seminary professor at the time and my students had challenged my thinking with some very incisive and penetrating questions. A young man whose approach to ministry reflected the anti-institutional disposition of the late 1960s and 1970s queried, "Do you think God is going to bypass the Church and use some other means to carry out His purposes in the world?"

What made this student's question, and others like it, so disturbing was that he was absolutely serious. Like me, he believed the Bible was the inspired Word of God. But his local church experience, although limited, was so negative that he interpreted

Scripture through a lens of disappointment and disillusionment. Furthermore, his nonreligious cultural experience—he was a relatively new Christian—had imbued the eyes of his heart with a pair of dark glasses. I soon concluded that when distorted religious experience is aligned with the values of the secular world, it always produces a lethal combination!

Although such questions were a threat at first, I soon appreciated those troubling and at times intense discussions. In reality, my student's questions were really statements of concern blended with valid doubts. As a result, I was driven back to our common source for ultimate answers—in this case, the book of Acts and the New Testament letters. Although Jesus came to lay the foundation for the Church (see Matt. 16:18), it is Luke's second report that dramatically profiles the birth and expansion of the Church, a discourse we have come to identify as the book of Acts (compare Luke 1:1-4 with Acts 1:1-11).

Furthermore, the New Testament letters, which were written to several of the local churches mentioned in Acts, give us an authentic perspective on what the writers expected to happen among believers in every local community. The books include lessons on how Christians should relate to God, to one another and to neighbors who do not understand or respond to the gospel, which is the good news that "Christ died for our sins according to the Scriptures, that he was buried, that he was raised on the third day according to the Scriptures" (1 Cor. 15:3-4).

I have always believed in the importance of the local church and ever since I became a Christian at age 16, I have been actively involved, both as a layperson and staff member. However, this new challenge had a dramatic impact upon my life. It was not just another exegetical and intellectual experience—although it was certainly that. Rather, it was a very challenging and life-changing experience! I came to appreciate and love the Church and its great potential in this world as never before, and I committed to do everything I could to help this unique God-created organism become all that God intended it to be.

My students and I launched into an exciting and adventurous journey. We went back to reexamine the beginning of the Church—starting with the Great Commission (see Matt. 28:19-20), and then looked carefully at the local churches scattered throughout the first-century world. How did New Testament leaders *make* disciples and then *teach* those disciples? What happened to those churches once they came into existence? We wanted to know.

Three things happened to me during this two- to three-year process. First, I wrote a book I never planned to write. It emerged out of my classroom experience and is titled *Sharpening the Focus of the Church*. Frankly, I never anticipated how God would use this material to help others around the world take a fresh look at the Church as it is described in the New Testament.

Second, in November 1972, my wife and I, and several families, started a church we never planned to start—the first Fellowship Bible Church in the Dallas Metroplex. Before *Sharpening the Focus of the Church* was published, I shared the basic principles recorded in the book with these families. Their response was immediate and urgent. They wanted to start a new church and invited me to be the founding pastor. At that time, I never anticipated that this church would eventually multiply into at least a dozen churches in the Dallas area and serve as a model for hundreds of other churches, both in the United States and throughout the world.

The third event affected my vocational life. The church grew rapidly leading me to make another decision I had not planned to make. I moved out of the sacred halls of learning to operate at the grassroots level as a church-planting pastor. Needless to say, this was quite a change after 13 years of working full time in a Bible college and seven years in a theological seminary. Although I certainly learned a lot as a professor, my real learning began when I started to apply the principles I had written about.

Early in my church-planting experience, I delivered a series of messages to my new and growing congregation titled "The Measure of a Church." This eventually became a book with the same title. What follows is a complete rewrite, in essence a brand-new publication, based on nearly 30 years of church-planting adventures. My prayer is that it will help you develop an even greater passion for the wonderful mystery of Christ that was unveiled more than 2,000 years ago: the Church of Jesus Christ.

CHAPTER 1

GOD'S MYSTERY REVEALED

I am excited about the Church—the great mystery that God has revealed. After all, this glorious reality was in the mind of God even before He created the world (see Eph. 1:4). In fact, in His divine plan we are already an eternal community, God's prized possession (see Eph. 1:14).

To carry out this divine plan within the framework of time, God sent His Son Jesus Christ to redeem us with His blood and to forgive our sins (see Eph. 1:7). As a result, someday, perhaps soon, believers from throughout time will be presented to Christ as His perfect Bride. What a glorious moment that will be as we celebrate that great event, the wedding of the Lamb (see Rev. 19:7). On that wonderful day we will be like Christ—"a radiant church, without stain or wrinkle or any other blemish" (Eph. 5:27).

In the meantime, we live in the here and now. All over the world God has called us to be His "workmanship, created in Christ Jesus to do good works" (Eph. 2:10). We are to reflect His character, which is His righteousness and holiness. It is clear that the Scriptures give us very specific criteria for evaluating the extent that we as His people are "mature, attaining to the whole measure of the fullness of Christ" (Eph. 4:13).

This measure of fullness is what our study in this book is all about! As believers, we certainly do not want to be like the Corinthians, who were "a poor reflection" of Jesus Christ. Someday, of course, we shall see our Lord face-to-face (see 1 Cor. 13:12). We will be like Christ "for we shall see him as he is" (1 John 3:2). However, the present challenge before us is to moment-by-moment and day-by-day be more and more conformed to His glorious image (see Rom. 12:1-2).

Thankfully, the Word of God makes very clear what the image of Christ is—and with God's help we can reflect that image in wonderful ways. We can begin to do this even before the trumpet sounds when we will all be changed and transported into His very presence (see 1 Cor. 15:52). The more we understand God's wonderful plan for the Church and the more we are involved in this process of spiritual growth, the more excited we will become about the Church of Jesus Christ! I know that I am, and I hope that you will be, too!

Defining the Church

Before we unfold God's plan for measuring a church, we need to define "church." In other words, what are we measuring?

It is my deep personal conviction that the primary sources for gaining this understanding are the books of the New Testament. Therefore, let's take a careful look at this amazing set of historical documents and what they declare about the revelation from God that Paul called the "mystery of Christ" (Eph. 3:4). When Paul wrote "to the saints in Ephesus" (Eph. 1:1) and the other churches in Asia,[1] he reminded them that this "*mystery* . . . was not made known to men in other generations as it has now been revealed by the Spirit to God's holy apostles and prophets" (Eph. 3:4-5).

What is this mystery? Paul went on to answer this question, even though some believing Jewish people had difficulty accepting his explanation. Perhaps they had trouble understanding Paul because the Gentiles were "excluded from citizenship in Israel and foreigners to the covenants of promise, without hope and without God in the world" (Eph. 2:12). But now, Paul insisted that both Jews and Gentiles were "members together of one body, and sharers together in the promise in Christ Jesus" (Eph. 3:6, see also Eph. 2:13-22).

While describing this amazing revelation, Paul maintained a spirit of great humility. He truly considered himself "less than the least of all God's people" (Eph. 3:8)—because of the way he had persecuted followers of Jesus Christ (see 1 Tim. 1:12-14). Yet God called him "to preach to the Gentiles the unsearchable riches of Christ" (Eph. 3:8). Paul never ceased to be amazed that, by God's grace, he was the one to proclaim this mystery, which he emphasized was revealed and embodied in the Church.

The Ekklesia of God

The Greek term "*ekklesia*" appears throughout the New Testament to describe the Church. Jesus used the word three times. The other 100 or so occurrences refer to people who had responded to the gospel and put their faith in the Lord Jesus Christ for eternal salvation. Furthermore, the term is used to describe both the universal Church and the local church. (See appendix A for a complete listing of verses that use the word "*ekklesia*.")

The Universal Church

Biblical authors used *ekklesia* approximately 20 times[2] to refer to the universal Church, which we can describe in two ways:

1. All first-century believers scattered throughout the Roman world.
2. All believers of all time who are members of the Body of Christ.

Let me illustrate: When Paul wrote to the Galatians and Corinthians, he confessed that as an unbeliever he had "persecuted the *church* of God" (Gal. 1:13; see also 1 Cor. 15:9; Phil. 3:6). Paul was obviously referring not only to the believers in Jerusalem where he began his attack on the Church, but to all followers of Christ in the Roman world. In his testimony before King Agrippa, he said that he "even went to foreign cities to persecute" those who had accepted Jesus Christ as the true Messiah (Acts 26:11).

However, Paul did not write exclusively about the first-century Church. He also included Christians throughout the ages. In Ephesians, his references to the Church seem to involve believers who become a part of the Body of Christ any time from Pentecost to that moment when the Church is removed from the world:

> And God placed all things under his feet and appointed him to be head over everything for the church, which is his body, the fullness of him who fills everything in every way (Eph. 1:22-23; see also Eph. 3:10-11,20-21; 5:23-25,27,29,32).

The Local Church

Although biblical writers used the term "*ekklesia*" to refer to all believers in Jesus Christ, both at a moment in time and throughout the Church age and into eternity, in most instances (82 to be exact) they used it to refer to believers who lived in specific geographical locations. In other words, in approximately 80 percent of the time the words "church" or "churches" were selected to refer to what we call "local churches" (see appendix A).

We must not, however, think of these "local churches" through the lenses of our twenty-first century structural models. In most instances, New Testament passages pertain to all professing believers in a particular city or community. For example, Luke cited "the church at Jerusalem" (Acts 8:1) and "the church at Antioch" (Acts 13:1). Describing Paul's first missionary journey, Luke referenced "each church" in "Lystra, Iconium and Antioch [Pisidian]" (Acts 14:21,23).

On his second missionary journey, Paul wrote to the "the *church* of the *Thessalonians*" (1 Thess. 1:1). However, Paul pluralized this term when he addressed the "the *churches* in Galatia" (Gal. 1:2). In the same letter, he mentioned "the *churches* of Judea" (Gal. 1:22). And in his first letter to the Corinthians, he sent greetings from "the *churches* in the province of Asia" (1 Cor. 16:19). In his second letter to the Corinthians, he used "the Macedonian *churches*" as an example of generosity (2 Cor. 8:1).

In each of these verses, the biblical writers named local congregations in various geographical areas–primarily villages, towns or cities. As it is today, churches in the first century were established in various population centers.

The word "*ekklesia*" actually means an "assembly," or "congregation," of people. However, New Testament writers used the word to describe Christians whether they were gathered together for worship or scattered throughout an area–in their homes, at work, shopping, visiting relatives or recreating at the local spa.

God's Design for the Local Church

What kind of relationships should exist among the followers of Jesus Christ? How are we to function? What should we look like to both believers and nonbelievers? What qualities reflect maturity? The answers to these questions reflect my concern in this book: the true measure of a local church.

New Testament writers most frequently used the words "disciples," "brothers" and "saints" (see appendix B) to describe local church participants. As with the term "*ekklesia*," each definition gives fresh insight as to why these terms were selected. Clearly the Church is made up of people who are followers of Jesus Christ, who have deep relationships with one another and who increasingly reflect who God is as they manifest the fruit of the Holy Spirit.

Disciples

The word "disciple" appears 30 times in Acts. Each time it applies to true followers of Jesus Christ. Interestingly, when Luke identified believers as disciples, he only did so in the context of local churches—not the universal Church (see appendix A). In fact, he used the term interchangeably when referring to local churches. For example, when Paul left on his second missionary journey, we read that "he [Paul] went through Syria and Cilicia, *strengthening the churches*" (Acts 15:41). When Paul left on his third journey, Luke recorded that he "traveled from place to place throughout the region of Galatia and Phrygia, *strengthening all the disciples*" (Acts 18:23).

The Gospel Records

When Matthew, Mark, Luke and John penned the Gospels, they identified as disciples all those who followed Jesus and listened to His teachings. The basic Greek word for "disciple," "*mathetes,*" literally means "a learner." That is why the term is used to describe the "disciples of John the Baptist" (Matt. 9:14, *NLT*); the "disciples of the Pharisees" (Mark 2:18); and the "disciples of Moses" (John 9:28). It follows naturally that those who followed and listened to Jesus' teaching were also identified as disciples of Jesus.

Though a large number of people claimed to be Jesus' learners, many of these so-called disciples turned their backs on the Savior when His demands became too great. For example, after Jesus had multiplied the loaves and fish for the huge crowd that had followed Him to the far shore of Galilee, He challenged a smaller group to accept Him as the Bread of Life. Not everyone welcomed the news. Some of the people became confused and disillusioned. John recorded that "many of his disciples turned back and no longer followed him" (John 6:66).

When we look carefully at the disciples of Jesus in the Gospel records, we will discover people who were never fully committed to Christ. In fact, most were disciples in name only. Even all of the 12 disciples (the apostles) eventually deserted Jesus. Judas, of course, betrayed the Lord, but the others fled when He was arrested (see Matt. 26:56).

The Book of Acts

When we encounter the word "disciples" in Acts, it takes on a much broader and deeper meaning.

The Presence of the Holy Spirit

As Luke picks up the rest of the story in Acts, Jesus had completed His redemptive plan. He had died for the sins of the world and had been raised from the dead. Those who followed this teacher and miracle worker prior to His crucifixion were hoping that He was the Messiah who had come to establish an earthly kingdom in Israel. In fact, this was still in the minds of the apostles just before Jesus ascended to heaven from the Mount of Olives. "Lord," they asked, "are you at this time going to restore the kingdom to Israel?" (Acts 1:6). At this moment, they still did not fully understand Jesus' redemptive work for the whole world. However, their limited knowledge about Jesus was about to change.

When the Holy Spirit descended on them with power on the Day of Pentecost, this relatively small group formed the core of the church.

After the Lord ascended, His disciples, numbering approximately 120, obeyed Jesus' command to wait in Jerusalem (see Acts 1:4, 13-14). When the Holy Spirit descended on them with power on the Day of Pentecost, this relatively small group formed the core of the church.

As with all true believers, they became members of the universal Church—the Body of Christ. "John baptized with water, but in a few days," He had told them, they would "be baptized with the Holy Spirit" (Acts 1:5). When this supernatural event took place, they began to understand why Jesus had really come into this world.

A Born-Again Experience

People who responded to the gospel message proclaimed by the apostles in Jerusalem became true followers of the risen and ascended Christ. They understood much more clearly what they had heard from the lips of Jesus. At that point, He was not only their teacher and they His learners, but He was also their Savior. They became His disciples in a new and much more meaningful way and were baptized into the Body of Christ by the Holy Spirit. That small band of born-again believers soon multiplied many times when 3,000 accepted Peter's message on the Day of Pentecost. They put their faith in the Lord Jesus Christ and were baptized (see Acts 2:41).[3]

Do not misunderstand. Not all who joined this expanding group of disciples suddenly became paragons of faith, virtue and holiness. But even then, as in every church today, some of these disciples matured quickly. Others took a longer period of time before they were able to truly "live a life worthy of the calling [that they had] received" (Eph. 4:1). This is why Jesus commissioned the apostles not only to "make disciples" (secure professions of faith) but also to teach these disciples everything He had taught them (see Matt. 28:19-20). In other words, it takes time and effort to produce mature, dedicated and committed disciples who measure up to God's standards. This is certainly evident in Luke's history of the Church as recorded in Acts.

Brothers

As the apostles began to take the Great Commission seriously, a different word was used to characterize these followers of Jesus Christ. The disciples were also called "brothers"—a concept that the authors of the New Testament turned to more frequently than any other when writing about those who became a part of the *ekklesia* of God (see Acts 1:16).

Both Generic and Specific

The Greek word *"adelphoi,"* translated as "brothers," or as "brethren," is often used generically to refer to both brothers and sisters in Christ. This type of reference appears in many languages. For example, in Spanish, the term *hermanos* (brothers) can be used to refer exclusively to men, or it can be used to refer to both men and women. Unfortunately, we have no equivalent word in the English language that describes both men and women. Consequently, when we read our Bibles, it is easy to always interpret brothers as masculine, but many times it includes both men and women.

As we have seen, the word "disciples" only appears in Acts. However, "brothers" can be found in Acts and many other New Testament books. In fact, in Acts believers are called brothers 32 times–almost the same number of times they are referred to as disciples (see appendix B). *Adelpoi*, or the singular *adelphos*, appears in the New Testament more than 200 times.

A Unique Family Term

"Brother" is a very intimate term that is used to describe these new disciples. It is a familial term that implies the people are blood brothers and sisters. However, when men and women put their faith in Jesus and became His disciples, they also became "brothers and sisters in Christ"–born of the seed of Abraham (see Gen. 12:2-3; Rom. 4:9-12). As Paul stated so clearly in his letter to the Romans, Abraham "is the father of all who believe" (Rom. 4:11). And in his letter to the Ephesians, he wrote that when we put our faith in Christ, we are born again into God's eternal family and become "members of God's household" (Eph. 2:19).

SAINTS

Another word that is used to describe born-again members of the Church is "saints" (*hagios* in Greek). It appears in the New

Testament nearly 50 times in this context and can also describe the Spirit of God. He is called the Holy (*hagios*) Spirit. Consequently, when New Testament writers selected the term "saints," they were depicting people who were holy in God's sight.

For example, Paul addressed the Corinthians as saints (see 2 Cor. 1:2), even though most of them were living anything but godly lives (see 1 Cor. 3:1-3). Yet, because of their faith in Jesus Christ and their true salvation experience, God viewed them through Christ's death and resurrection as perfectly *hagios,* or holy.

This is the way God sees each of us. If He did not, no one could be saved. This is why the doctrine of salvation by grace through faith and not by works is so important. None of us by our own strength can live a perfect life nor can we qualify on our own to gain entrance into God's eternal kingdom. As Paul informed the Galatians, we can never be saved or justified by trying to keep the law (see Gal. 2:16). Only Jesus Christ kept the law of God perfectly, and that is why He is our Savior.

However, even though we cannot reach this standard in this life, it is still God's will for all of us to become holy as God is holy (see 1 Peter 1:15-16). We are to renew our minds—not to "conform any longer to the pattern of this world," but to "be transformed" (Rom. 12:2). Put another way, we are to rid ourselves of the sinful acts of the flesh and to manifest the fruit of the Holy Spirit in all of our relationships (see Gal. 5:16-26).

Guiding Principles

Principle 1. When measuring a church, we can only evaluate a local, visible body of believers.

The universal Church is a wonderful reality. Even at this moment, it exists in all parts of the world—all believers everywhere are members. However, as the *Bride of Christ* (another name for the universal Church), God is preparing all believers of all time for that great moment in the future when we will be presented to the Lord at what New Testament writers called the Wedding Supper of the Lamb (see Rev. 19:7-8). Only God, of course, knows who true believers are. In fact, God chose us and glorified us in Christ before the creation of the world (see Rom. 8:30; Eph. 1:4).

God, of course, can measure the universal Church, whether at a moment in history, throughout history, or on into eternity. However, from a human point of view, we can only measure what we see and experience. Consequently, God has given us many illustrations in the New Testament to assist us in measuring our own churches—wherever we exist in the world. Although first-century churches existed in various cultures far removed from our own, what we read about them yields powerful guiding principles that transcend cultural boundaries. That is why we can identify these principles as "supracultural."

Principle 2. When measuring a church, we must measure functions, not forms or structures.

In actuality, the Scriptures give us very little information regarding the forms in New Testament churches. This is by divine design. If God had made church structures absolute, throughout history, He would have locked believers into a particular culture. Biblical functions, however, are supracultural, and when we examine the way our churches are functioning, we can then evaluate whether or not our forms are appropriate and adequate.

As we proceed through this study, we will look specifically at the functions God has outlined for local churches and what these functions should produce in terms of mature believers. The results of these functions, when carried out properly, will in turn provide criteria for measuring our local churches in the twenty-first century. In essence, these criteria are the guiding principles located at the end of each chapter.

Principle 3. When measuring a church, we must have a comprehensive understanding of biblical discipleship.

True disciples are not just learners or followers of a great moral teacher named Jesus Christ. They are born-again believers, people who have put their faith in Jesus Christ as the Son of God and have experienced redemption.

This does not mean that all true disciples are mature disciples. As Jesus commanded, we are not only to "make disciples of all nations" but we are also to teach "them to obey everything" He has commanded (Matt. 28:19-20).

Luke recorded a beautiful illustration of how the Great Commission can be carried out. On Paul and Barnabas's first missionary journey, they proclaimed the Word of the Lord in Derbe and won (literally "made") a large number of *disciples.* Luke recorded that they then "returned to Lystra, Iconium and Antioch [where they had also made a large number of disciples]." As they once again traveled through these cities, they were "*strengthening* the disciples and encouraging them to remain true to the faith" (Acts 14:21-22).

Principle 4. When measuring a church, we must evaluate the degree to which the true disciples in that church are functioning as a family.

The family, or household, metaphor takes us back to the creation story. We read that God said, "Let us make man [humankind] in our image, in our likeness" (Gen. 1:26).

Stanley Grenz captured this great truth when he wrote:

> The God we know is the Triune One—the Father, Son and Holy Spirit united together in perfect love. Because God

> is "community"—fellowship shared among the Father, Son and Spirit—the creation of humankind in the divine image must be related to humans in fellowship with each other. God's own character can only be mirrored by humans who love after the manner of the perfect love, which lies at the heart of the Triune God.[4]

The relationship enjoyed by Adam and Eve was possible because *together* they could experience the fellowship that existed in the eternal Trinity. But sin marred this beautiful relationship and the relationships that God intended for their offspring. The human family was destined for pain, tension, jealousy

In order to restore us to fellowship, God designed and unfolded a wonderful mystery, the Church.

and all the other evil works of the flesh. Consequently, this couple's sin, of course, spread to the whole human race (see Rom. 5:12-14).

But God had a wonderful plan of restoration. In the fullness of time, He sent His Son into the world. The "Word became flesh and made his dwelling among us" (John 1:14). Jesus Christ died for the sins of the world in order to enable us to once again be in fellowship with God and with one another.

In order to restore us to fellowship, God designed and unfolded a wonderful mystery, the Church—a group of disciples who were not only born-again learners but brothers and sisters in Christ who form one body, regardless of our gender and ethnic and economic backgrounds. We are meant to be a family—the household of God.

"How does this happen?" Grenz asked in his book *Created for Community*. His answer captures the essence of true fellowship and community:

> The Holy Spirit is the one who transforms us from a collection of individuals into a fellowshipping people. In conversion, he draws us out of our isolation and alienation. In so doing, he knits us together as one people. Indeed, there arises among us a oneness which is nothing less than the unity of the Spirit himself (Eph. 4:3).[5]

Principle 5: When measuring a church, we must evaluate the degree to which believers are reflecting the fruit of the Spirit in their relationships with one another.

When Paul wrote "to the churches in Galatia" (Gal. 1:2), he gave us a very comprehensive criterion for measuring holiness in a local community of believers. We are to consider the degree to which they reflect the fruit of the Spirit, which, according to Paul, "is love, joy, peace, patience, kindness, goodness, faithfulness, gentleness and self-control" (Gal. 5:22-23).

The apostle was contrasting these Christlike qualities with the "acts of the sinful nature" which he outlines as "sexual immorality, impurity and debauchery; idolatry and witchcraft; hatred, discord, jealousy, fits of rage, selfish ambition, dissension, factions and envy; drunkenness, orgies, and the like" (Gal. 5:19-21).

Note two important things about this passage. First, Paul was in essence contrasting holy living with unholy living. We must remember that the third person of the Godhead is frequently identified as the Holy (*hagios)* Spirit—and here Paul is describing those qualities that reflect God's power and presence in our lives once we are "baptized by one Spirit into one body" (1 Cor. 12:13).

Second, the same qualities that reflect God's holiness are, for the most part, relational in their outworkings. They are not feelings that flow out of individual believers' lives when each of us is "filled with the Spirit." Rather, when, *as a local body of believers,* we "live by the Spirit" (Gal. 5:16) and "keep in step with the Spirit" (Gal. 5:25), we will love one another. As we do, we will experience joy, peace, unity and oneness. We will demonstrate patience and kindness in our relationships. We will treat one another with goodness, faithfulness, gentleness and self-control. This is the fruit of the Holy Spirit.

By contrast, Christians who live carnal lives according to their sinful flesh (see 1 Cor. 3:1-3) will reflect the acts of the sinful nature in their relationships—such as sexual immorality, impurity and debauchery. Rather than loving one another and demonstrating patience and kindness that lead to peace, unity and oneness, there will be acts of "hatred, discord, jealousy, and even fits of rage." There will be "selfish ambition, dissension, factions and envy."[6]

Unfortunately, the *corporate* nature of these contrasts in Paul's letter to the Galatian churches has often been overlooked and even misinterpreted.[7] We have tended to individualize Paul's directives, which has often led us to emotionalize the fruit of the Spirit. This can lead to false expectations and even disillusionment in our personal experiences. However, when we understand the relational and communal focus that Paul had in mind, we have a clearer picture and can better evaluate a local body of believers. We can discern as to whether or not that band of believers demonstrates *the fruit of the Holy Spirit* or the acts of the sinful nature. In essence, the positive qualities are a reflection of

God's holiness and as saints we are to become more and more conformed to the image of Jesus Christ. This is certainly what Peter had in mind when he exhorted Christians to be holy because God is holy (see 1 Pet. 1:15).

Thinking and Growing Together

As you approach this assignment, be careful to come with a nonjudgmental attitude. To avoid judging others, include yourself in this evaluation. To what extent are *you* a maturing disciple?

1. As you observe the overall functions and behaviors of believers in your church, to what extent are they becoming mature disciples? Are they men and women who are *growing* in their knowledge of the Word of God and *obeying* everything Jesus has taught them?
2. To what extent are the believers in your church operating as a loving, unified family, being "devoted to one another in brotherly love" (Rom. 12:10)? To help you carry out this exercise, look specifically at the other "one another" injunctions outlined in chapter 8, pages 189-190.
3. To what extent are the believers in your church reflecting the fruit of the Spirit in all of their relationships? In other words, to what extent are they saints who increasingly reflect the righteous and holy life of Jesus Christ?

Notes

1. The phrase "to the saints at Ephesus" does not appear in the earliest Greek manuscripts. It was probably added later since Ephesus was where Paul's extensive outreach to Asia began. During his two-year ministry at the lecture hall of Tyrannus, Luke recorded, "that all the Jews and Greeks who lived in the province of Asia heard the word of the Lord" (Acts 19:10). This is why Paul's letter to the Ephesians is often classified as a circular letter. It was no doubt read first in the church in Ephesus and then in the churches in Smyrna, Pergamum, Thyatira, Sardis, Philadelphia and Laoedicea, which the apostle John later identified as the "seven churches in the province of Asia" (Rev. 1:4). This also may explain why Paul identified the Church in a universal sense in this letter, rather than in a local sense.
2. I have used the term "approximately" since it is at times difficult to differentiate whether the authors of Scripture were using "*ekklesia*" to refer to the universal Church or the local church. However, as you will note in appendix A, in most instances, it is very clear.
3. It is difficult to tell when the 11 apostles became born-again believers. Was it when Jesus "breathed on them and said, 'Receive the Holy Spirit'" (John 20:22)? Did Thomas, who was absent when Jesus said this, become a true disciple after he saw the nail prints in Jesus' hands and the wound in His side and confessed, "My Lord and my God" (John 20:28)? Only God knows the answers to these questions. One thing is sure: They were definitely true disciples on the Day of Pentecost.
4. Stanley J. Grenz, *Created for Community* (Grand Rapids, MI: Baker Books, 1998), p. 80.
5. Ibid., p. 214.
6. As we will see in chapter 5, the Corinthians represent a church that was not reflecting "the fruit of the Spirit" but rather the "acts of the sinful nature."
7. Paul's letter was addressed "to the *churches* in Galatia" (Gal. 1:2)–that is, *communities* of believers. Paul continued this corporate emphasis by using the second person plural in the Greek text throughout this passage we have just examined. "Do not [as a body] use *your* freedom [in your relationships] to indulge the sinful nature," Paul wrote. "Rather," he continued, "*serve one another* in love" (Gal. 5:13). To carry out this corporate directive, we are to "*live* by the Spirit" in all of our relationships. And if we "live by the Spirit," we are to "keep in step with the Spirit." And if we "keep in step with the Spirit," we will "not become conceited, provoking and envying *each other*"(Gal. 5:25-26).

C H A P T E R 2

Metaphors That Measure

As we have closed out the twentieth century and have entered a new millennium, I have been intrigued with the metaphors that authors have used to measure a church.

For example, one book uses a luxury hotel, complete with its state-of-the-art facilities and unparalleled service. Applying this metaphor in the church environment, the authors suggest visitors should find quality in fellowship functions, building designs and believers' spiritual lives.

Another church growth book suggests we look to majestic redwoods to illustrate how to measure successful churches—churches that are dynamic, relational, natural and big!

BIBLICAL METAPHORS

Utilizing metaphors to describe and measure the Church is as old as the Church itself. We certainly have a biblical precedent for this picturesque language. In fact, Paul Minear contends that there are 96 analogies in the New Testament that help illustrate what the church should be.[1] In Peter's first letter to the communities of faith "scattered throughout Pontus, Galatia, Cappadocia, Asia and Bithynia" (1 Pet. 1:1), he relied upon a number of metaphors to communicate his message. He identified believers as "living stones" in a "spiritual house" (1 Pet. 2:5). The Church is called a "holy priesthood" that offers spiritual sacrifices to God. We are also a "royal priesthood" and a "holy nation" (1 Pet. 2:9).

A Field

The apostle Paul identified the Church as "God's field" (1 Cor. 3:5-9). This agricultural metaphor beautifully correlates with Jesus' parable of the sower (see Matt. 13:1-23; Mark 4:1-20; Luke 8:4-15). Though the Holy Spirit had not yet revealed the "mystery of Christ" to "God's holy apostles and prophets" (Eph. 3:4-5; see also Acts 1:6-8 and Eph. 3:2-12), Jesus was figuratively laying the groundwork for the Church He had come to build (see Matt. 16:18). A church that measures up to God's standard "hears the word and understands it" and "produces a crop, yielding a hundred, sixty or thirty times what was sown" (Matt. 13:23). This multiplication process is based not just on quantity but also on quality. Jesus envisioned lives that would be deeply rooted in the rich soil of the Word of God and that would become spiritually productive.

A Building

Paul also used an architectural metaphor: He identified the Corinthians as "God's building" (1 Cor. 3:9). Paul had laid a foundation, which is Jesus Christ—and other spiritual leaders who followed him built upon that foundation (see 1 Cor. 3:10-11).

In his Ephesian letter, Paul expanded on this metaphor: He stated that the Church is "built on the *foundation* of the apostles and prophets, with Christ Jesus Himself as the *chief cornerstone*. In him, the *whole building* is joined together and rises to become a holy temple in the Lord" (Eph. 2:20-21).

It is interesting to see that when writing to the Corinthians, Paul presented Jesus Christ as the foundation. When writing to the Ephesians, he presented those Jesus equipped to launch the Church as a part of the foundation.[2]

The apostle Peter used the same building metaphor but expanded its application. He presented Jesus Christ as the "living Stone" and established all believers as "living stones" that are "being built into a spiritual house" (1 Pet. 2:4-5).

A Body

An anatomical illustration is one of Paul's most graphic metaphors for the Church and one that is exclusively his own. He characterized God's people as the *Body* of Christ. In his letters to the Romans, the Corinthians, the Ephesians and the Colossians, he penned the Greek word *soma*—which is translated "body"—more than 30 times to illustrate how the Church should function. Approximately half of the time, he referred to the many parts of the human body; in the other half, he applied the term to the Church, the Body of Christ.[3]

THE LUXURY HOTEL

Biblical writers substantiate the value of metaphors—a variety of word pictures—when illustrating the church. In fact, the Scriptures also demonstrate that no one analogy can fully describe this unique, supernatural organism.

It is refreshing, then, to see today's authors use contemporary metaphors to describe the church. However, we must care-

It is refreshing to see today's authors use contemporary metaphors to describe the church. However, we must carefully choose how we use these analogies.

fully choose how we use these analogies. For example, as I pen these words, my wife and I have just spent a week in one of the most luxurious recreation destinations in the world, the magnificent Atlantis Resort in the Bahamas. I was invited to participate in a conference in the church of a pastor whom I have known for years. To express his appreciation for my ministry, he and his elders wanted my wife and me to stay in this wonderful five-star hotel in Nassau. What a pleasurable experience! Elaine and I never felt so pampered.

Although the luxury metaphor communicates excellence in service, which is certainly a biblical value, in most cultures of the world it also communicates excess, materialism, glitz, pampered guests and indulgence. In many respects, it also communicates what we can receive—not what we can give! Jesus told His disciples that He "did not come to be served, but to serve" (Matt. 20:28). Moreover, Paul exhorted the believers in the church in Philippi that their "attitude should be the same as Christ Jesus." They were to also become servants (see Phil. 2:5)!

Please understand that I have elaborated on the luxury hotel metaphor not to be overly critical but to illustrate why it is important to carefully choose our examples and criteria for measuring a church.

Sacrifice and Service

I enjoy staying in a quality hotel, but I have serious difficulty using such an experience to illustrate what a church should be. Indeed, the service is always exquisite—but is such pampering the kind of experience that Jesus had in mind for the church? On one occasion, He said to His disciples, "If anyone would come after me, he must deny himself and take up his cross daily and follow me" (Luke 9:23).

Staying in a luxury hotel is certainly a refreshing vacation—but should not be a daily or weekly occurrence. If I am going to function as Christ wants me to, I must be devoted to others in brotherly love and honor others above myself (see Rom. 12:10). This means I must sacrifice my own desires and serve others. I must "share with God's people who are in need" and "practice hospitality" (Rom. 12:13), which is another form of unselfishness. I must "rejoice with those who rejoice" and "mourn with those who mourn" (Rom. 12:15), which means that I must share in others' painful experiences as well as in their joys and pleasures. And I must accept others "just as Christ accepted" us (Rom. 15:7)—regardless of the other person's racial, ethnic, economic or cultural background.

These are just a few of the many exhortations that God has given all believers. When we apply these exhortations in our lives, they will enable us to fully function as members of the Body of Jesus Christ. Many of these experiences are joyful—or bring joy once we have been obedient. But in many instances, we must take up our crosses daily and obey Jesus Christ.

False Impressions

There is, of course, no perfect metaphor to illustrate the Church. This is why Paul and other biblical writers used so many. Though I find books such as the one that includes the luxury hotel metaphor to be stimulating reading and recommend them to any Christian leader, we must carefully evaluate the cultural implications. The weaknesses in the luxury metaphor can easily override its strengths. It can give false impressions regarding the true measure of a church.

In our efforts to provide a quality church experience which will impress and attract twenty-first-century people, we must understand what God says this qualitative experience should be. When we discover these standards, we will see that the criteria reflect the character of the church in Jerusalem in its most successful moments. We will learn that it falls perfectly in synch with the times they enjoyed the favor of all the people—which certainly includes nonbelievers, since we read that "the Lord added to their number daily those who were being saved" (Acts 2:47). A church that measures up to God's criteria will attract people no matter *where* they live in the world or *when* they inhabit planet Earth.

THE BIGGER THE BETTER

Let's also take a close look at the majestic-redwood metaphor. Again, it brings forth positive biblical values, such as incredible strength and stability. Like a redwood, a church should be an organism that is deeply rooted and stands the tests of time and nature, such as storms, weather changes and forest fires. In fact, some redwoods still alive today were towering upward when Jesus Christ walked the earth more than 2,000 years ago. For miles around, everyone can appreciate the redwood's grandeur and visibility. Looking upon these towering trees is an awesome and overwhelming experience.

On the other hand, this analogy implies *mega*proportions that overshadow and dwarf smaller species that may be just as alive and dynamic. In fact, while reflecting on this analogy, I met a young pastor who had started a new church. Though his congregation had reached an attendance of more than 400 people, his church sat in the shadow of a "giant redwood"—a megachurch that attracted about 12,000 attendees a week.

Predictably, pastors and other Christian leaders are enamored with the megachurch. Why is it so successful? What is its secret to such growth? How can I duplicate what *that* pastor has accomplished? Unfortunately, few Christian leaders know about smaller communities of believers that flourish—even in the shadow of these giant ministries. I have used the term "flourish" since the average attendance at a church in America hovers between 100 and 150 people. The relatively new church this young pastor was leading had already reached four times as many people than the average church reaches. To add to its success, this pastor's church attained its above average attendance while functioning near a church that is 30 times larger and almost identical in its belief system. This smaller church was flourishing!

Why am I making this comparison? Am I being critical of the megachurch? Absolutely not! The church in Jerusalem in its early days could certainly be defined as a megachurch since at one point it included almost 100,000 people. The congregation in Ephesus must also have been enormous. In other words, size is definitely not the issue. However, the bigness aspect of this metaphor can easily be misinterpreted as the true measure of a church! Furthermore, if we are not careful, this metaphor can elevate the importance of structure (the building)—like a redwood, the larger the structure the more visible it is. This metaphor can also misdirect us toward measuring a church by its multiplicity of programs, rather than by how the body functions.

Please, do not misunderstand my point. Bigness and true spiritual maturity are not mutually exclusive. We certainly can have both. I have the wonderful privilege of pastoring a megachurch in Plano, Texas: Fellowship Bible Church North. Moreover, a number of branch churches I have helped start in the Dallas area have become megachurches, each with 4,000 to 5,000 attendees. I would hope, however, that all of these churches are not just becoming *big* but have as their goal *the true measure of a church*: "Attaining to the whole measure of the fullness of Christ" (Eph. 4:13).

"Agreed!" you say. But should we not value external beauty and quality? Absolutely! Should we not emphasize visibility in the community? Definitely! In fact, as I pen these words, our leadership team is brainstorming this very issue: How do we let people know where we meet using effective lighting, signage and other techniques? When people find us, we want them to see a place that is characterized by quality and service. However, all of this *must* be a cultural means to reach a supracultural goal—to produce disciples who are willing to take up their crosses and follow Jesus Christ!

Beware of Faulty Presuppositions

These cautions lead to a more fundamental observation. I am concerned about a presuppositional issue that has led many church leaders to evaluate church success inappropriately, at least to some degree. It has been suggested that to be successful church planters in the new century, we must draw a new map.

In too many cases, however, this new map emerges amidst a new cultural wilderness. Consequently, the focus rests upon our existential experience with Jesus—who is certainly recognized as a man of history, the founder of Christianity and a great model—rather than on the unequivocal fact that Jesus Christ is the incarnate Son of God (God come in human flesh) and that He is the only way to eternal salvation.

Perhaps what is more disturbing are suggestions that when talking to seekers (unbelievers who might be interested in the gospel message), we should separate the name "Christ" from the name "Jesus." Some have also recommended that we avoid using the name "Christ" in our culture as a way to avoid communicating a concept of historical Christianity that is ecclesiastical and repugnant to the contemporary mind. Though I certainly believe wholeheartedly in Paul's commitment to be all things to all people in order to win them to Christ, even in our use of language, I cannot conceive of Paul dropping the names "Christ," "Lord," "Son of God," "King" and "Savior" from his evangelistic vocabulary.

In summary, this *new map* seems to focus more on historical and cultural sources than on revealed truth as it is recorded in the New Testament. This can lead to criteria for measuring success that have elements that are out of harmony with God's will for the Church.

Ecclesiological Flaws

Although I have deeply appreciated the number of books that have been written about the Church in recent years, I am also disturbed by the fact that some of these writings tend to be more pragmatic than biblical. The same is true of seminars that are designed to help leaders grow a successful church. I have often heard people say that they had attended seminars on church growth. They go on to tell how everyone there seemed to believe the Bible was the Word of God, but few leaders ever opened the Bible—or very seldom ever quoted from it. Their suggestions and ideas came more from pragmatic experience—what works—rather than first and foremost from biblical functions and principles.

Stanley Grenz, in his provocative book *Renewing the Center*, summarized some assessments on the state of the Church that appeared in *Christianity Today* about the time we entered the new millennium. Though perhaps overstated in some respects, his observations are worth noting and comparing to biblical standards for measuring a church:

> Some churches are restructuring congregational life in a manner that, perhaps even unbeknown to them, takes its cue more from the nation's business schools than from the Bible. Others are blindly and unquestionably catering to the contemporary consumerist mentality. Many evangelicals have substituted therapy for salvation, thereby "exchanging the language of Scripture for the language of *Psychology Today*," to cite Donald McCullough's disquieting appraisal. But above all, evangelicals today are falling prey to wholesale cultural accommodation.[4]

The contemporary metaphors I have cited in this chapter help illustrate my point: The analogies and contemporary illustrations many people use to describe success certainly reflect our society's standard for measuring a church. This tells us that our philosophy of ministry *does matter* because it affects the way we *do church* and the way we tell others how to do church. And it certainly affects the way we measure our activities and the results of those activities—the primary focus of this book.

SUPERNATURAL ARCHITECTURE

In his book *Supernatural Architecture,* Stan DeKovan makes a very important statement: "If the theological mandate of growth and the patterns of the Word of God are not adequately followed, one may produce a facsimile of a church without producing 'The Church' which would be in accordance with the will and purpose of God."[5] DeKovan later elaborates:

> To build a church, one must fully understand what should be the end result of that church. And although there can be great flexibility in terms of overall structure, there are certain characteristics of a truly New Testament church that must be a part of what is built in our modern society. These principles, which must be applied with flexibility and contextualized in modern culture, can be the foundation for seeing the Church become everything that God intended.[6]

Although I have difficulty with some of DeKovan's conclusions, I agree wholeheartedly with his statements, which generate some very basic questions: What does God intend the Church to be? What is the end-result we are trying to produce? What are God's standards for measurement?

We can only determine the answers to these questions by looking carefully at strengths and weaknesses of the first-century churches and at what New Testament writers outline as a true measure of a church. This is my goal in this book. I sincerely invite you to evaluate the degree to which I have achieved this purpose.

Guiding Principles

Principle 1. When measuring a church, we must look to the Scriptures as our final authority in faith and practice.

It is no secret that some Christian leaders are questioning whether or not all of the Scriptures are divinely inspired. When this happens, it opens the door to a diversity of interpretations that become more man centered than God centered. In setting up a standard for a successful church, we can become more sociological than theological. Pragmatics (what works) drive our thinking more than the inspired supracultural principles that emerge from a thorough exegetical study of the Bible.

Do not misunderstand. I am not suggesting a view of inspiration that ignores the human elements of the Scriptures or the cultural dynamics in the first century. God used each author's unique personality, experience, cultural background, education, research and other life experiences. Rather, I am advocating an approach to the Bible that reflects Paul's historical view of the Old Testament as well as his prophetic view of the New Testament. After encouraging Timothy to continue to practice what he had learned from a child about "the holy Scriptures," Paul went on to state:

> All Scripture is God-breathed and is useful for teaching, rebuking, correcting and training in righteousness, so that the man of God may be thoroughly equipped for every good work (2 Tim. 3:16-17).

We might paraphrase and apply Paul's statement in this way:

> All Scripture is God-breathed and is useful for discovering a divine criteria for determining the degree to which our local churches are measuring up to God's standard.

Principle 2. When measuring a church, we must have a clear understanding of the centrality of the *ekklesia* in God's scheme.

Having studied the Church from Scripture for a number of years and having attempted to apply these concepts in multiple church plants, I have come to the conclusion that the doctrine of ecclesiology [what the Bible says about the "Church"] is central in both understanding the new covenant and in growing and maturing in our individual Christian lives. I firmly believe that this doctrine is the glue that holds the New Testament together. After all, the Gospel writers recorded what Jesus said and did to lay the foundation for the Church. Luke's historical record in the book of Acts is a story of church planting throughout the Roman world, as he unfolded Jesus' prophetic declaration that He would build His Church (see Matt. 16:18). The greatest sources of standards used to measure a church are the letters in the New Testament that were written to these churches or to the men, such as Timothy and Titus, who were establishing these churches.

In essence, the New Testament is the story of the Church. When we understand the nature of the Church, we can properly interpret and apply all other doctrines more adequately—the doctrines about God, Christ, the Holy Spirit, man, salvation—and even eschatology, the doctrine that outlines the consummation of human history. In other words, a proper view of the Church in a very real sense becomes the organizing center for doing all theological studies.

Grenz developed this idea very comprehensively and conclusively in his excellent book titled *Theology for the Community of God*. Though he gave a broad definition of "community," it is clear that the Church was at the heart and center of his thinking when he wrote:

> "Community" is important as an integrated motif for theology . . . because it is central to the message of the

> Bible. From the narratives of the primordial garden which open the curtain on the biblical story to the vision of white-robed multitudes inhabiting the new earth with which it concludes, the drama of the Scriptures speaks of community. Taken as a whole the Bible asserts that God's program is directed to the bringing into being of community in the highest sense—a reconciled people, living within a renewed creation, and enjoying the presence of their Redeemer.[7]

Principle 3. When measuring a church, we must make sure that we have not allowed value shifts in our culture to cause us to reinterpret scriptural criteria in order to accommodate nonbiblical trends.

People can easily misunderstand this principle. I am not suggesting that we ignore cultural shifts in our society. If I did, I would be ignoring Jesus' approach to ministry. When He ministered to the woman at the well, He adjusted His communication style to bring her to a knowledge of the truth—that He could indeed forgive her sins because He was the Son of God.

To ignore culture and how people think would also be to ignore Paul's approach to ministry. He was always free to adjust his methodology to meet special human needs. This is what he meant when he said, "I have become all things to all men so that by all possible *means* I might save some" (1 Cor. 9:22).

Understand, of course, that Paul never compromised the supracultural truths of Scripture, not even in his choice of methods. At the same time, he never confused cultural methodology with supracultural principles. It was this theological insight that enabled him to uncompromisingly say, "To the Jews I became like a Jew, to win the Jews. . . . To those not having the law I became like one not having the law . . . so as to win those not having the law" (1 Cor. 9:20-21).

What we must *not* do, which is the true meaning of the principle just defined, is allow cultural shifts in values to cause us to reinterpret scriptural directives to accommodate those cultural changes in our society.

THINKING AND GROWING TOGETHER

1. What have you noticed about the way church success is measured when Christian leaders focus more on what works (pragmatic values) rather than on biblical directives and functions (biblical principles)?
2. What have you noticed in the lives of Christians who do not have a clear understanding of how God's plan for *personal* Christian growth is related to His plan for *corporate* Christian growth and maturity? For example, what happens to Christians who are consistently disconnected from a functioning body of believers?
3. Can you think of some areas in which you believe the Church has reinterpreted Scripture to include cultural values that actually compromise God's standards?

Notes

1. Paul S. Minear, *Images of the Church in the New Testament* (Philadelphia: The Westminster Press, 1960), pp. 268-269.
2. Here we see that no one metaphor describes the Church in all its glory. Furthermore, Paul used and mixed metaphors creatively to illustrate the Church and how it functions.
3. Here are the references where the term "body" (*soma*) illustrates a properly functioning church: Romans 12:4-5; 1 Corinthians 12:12-27; Ephesians 1:23; 2:16; 4:4,12,16; 5:23; 5:30; Colossians 1:18; 2:19; 3:15.

4. Stanley J. Grenz, *Renewing the Center* (Grand Rapids, MI: Baker Books, 2000), p. 12.
5. Stan DeKovan, *Supernatural Architecture: Preparing the Church for the 21st Century* (Colorado Springs, CO: Wagner Institute Publications, 1997), p. 18.
6. Ibid., p. 33.
7. Stanley J. Grenz, *Theology for the Community of God* (Nashville, TN: Broadman and Holman Publishers, 1994), p. 30.

C H A P T E R 3

THE PERFECT MEASUREMENT

More was written in the last decade of the twentieth century than ever before about how to grow successful churches. Often these books were penned by church-planting pastors who told about their own successes.

We need these stories. They are inspiring and motivating. They include practical ideas and suggestions for doing church in the twenty-first century. For example, Rick Warren has written a stimulating book titled *The Purpose-Driven Church*.[1] For the most part, this book is *his* story. Committed to the message of the Bible and the Great Commission, Warren and his associates have built a great church in Southern California, and we can learn many things from their experiences.

More recently, Robert Lewis, with the help of Rob Wilkins, has told the story of Fellowship Bible Church in Little Rock,

Arkansas. Specifically, Lewis recounts testimonies of people whose lives have been impacted for Christ as a result of the church's outreach to the community. I was particularly interested in this book because this influence grew out of the ministry of the original Fellowship Bible Church in Dallas. Several families from this church we began in 1972 moved to Little Rock and launched another dynamic ministry. Their success is featured in an inspiring book titled *The Church of Irresistible Influence*.[2]

There are many churches that have become successful and influential in recent years. Identified by Leadership Network as "teaching churches," we need to learn from their stories. However, we must always read these personal accounts with an eye to scriptural principles. The only safe and sure criteria for measuring the success of our churches must come from the pen of the inspired authors of the Bible because, unlike current

When determining how to measure our churches according to God's standard, Paul's letters are absolutely essential.

accounts about local churches, the New Testament is *not* a record of success stories. Rather, it presents the strengths and weaknesses of the first-century church. In some instances, there were many more weaknesses than strengths.

The Master Church Planter

When determining how to measure our churches according to God's standard, Paul's letters are absolutely essential. We know more about his church-planting efforts than those of any other apostle.

The First Journey (see figure 3.1)

On his first missionary journey, Paul and Barnabas established churches in southern Galatia (see Acts 13:1–14:28). After successfully making disciples in Antioch of Pisidia, as well as in Iconium, Lystra and Derbe, they circled back to help these believers become established in their faith. As Paul and Barnabas moved from city to city, they appointed qualified elders in each church. The entire trip lasted about three years (A.D. 46-48). (I have included a chronological time line of Paul's life and ministry in appendix D).

The Second Journey (see figure 3.2)

After returning to Antioch of Syria, Paul developed an intense desire to revisit the churches he and Barnabas had planted on their first journey. Paul began the trip alone, going "through Syria and Cilicia, *strengthening the churches*" (Acts 15:41). Silas evidently joined Paul in Lystra and became his new missionary companion. Timothy also united with the team. These three men, along with Luke, expanded their ministry into Europe, where some of the most prominent churches mentioned in the New Testament were planted, including congregations in Philippi, Thessalonica and Corinth.

After spending at least a year and a half in Corinth, Paul again returned to his home base in Antioch of Syria. He stopped briefly in Ephesus but promised to return (see Acts 18:11-22). This second journey, like the first, lasted about three years (A.D. 49-52).

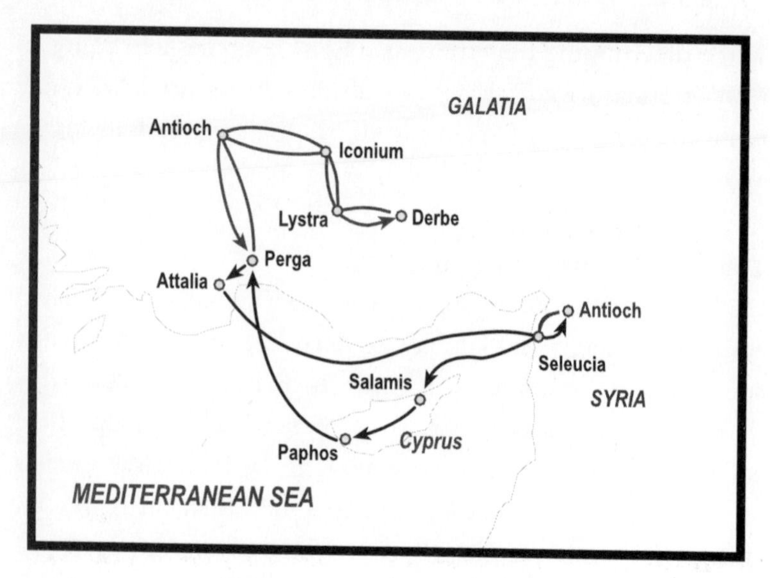

Figure 3.1 Paul's First Journey

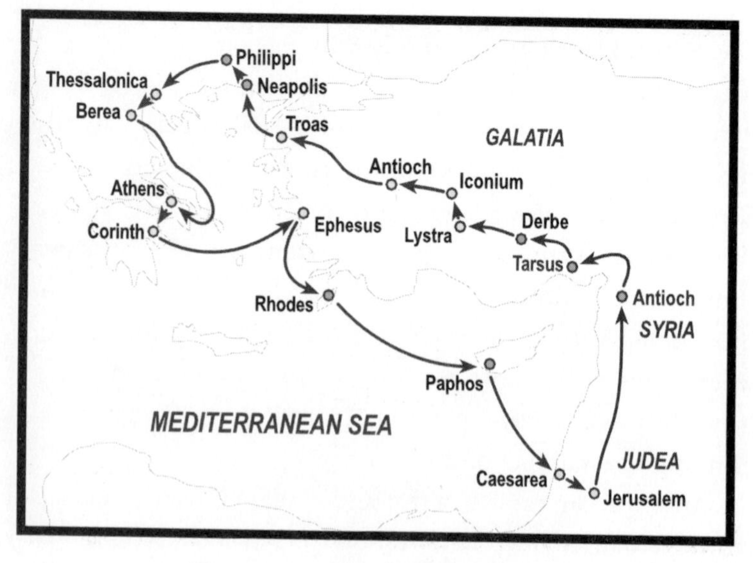

Figure 3.2 Paul's Second Journey

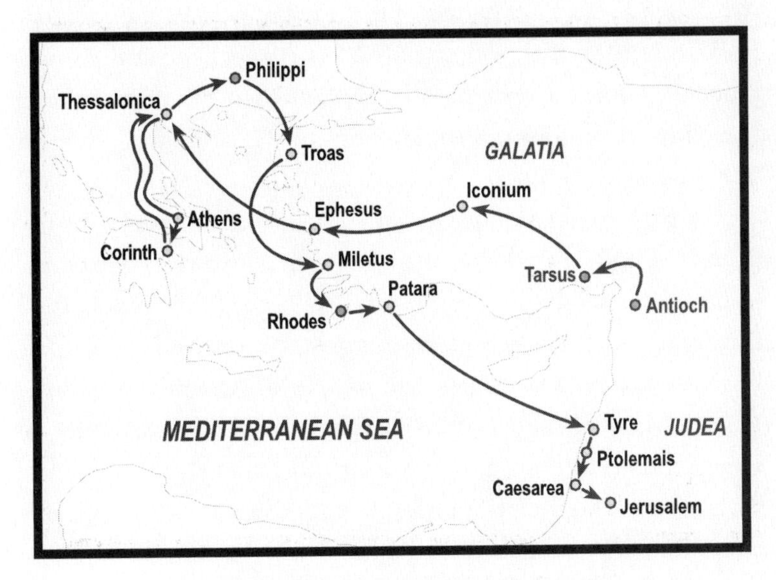

Figure 3.3 Paul's Third Journey

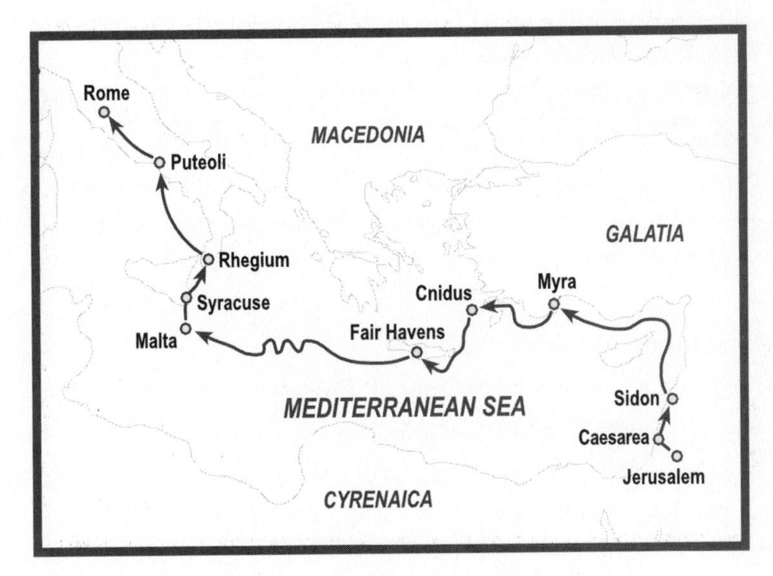

Figure 3.4 Paul's Journey to Rome

The Third Journey (see figure 3.3)

After spending a brief period of time in Antioch, Paul once again became burdened to follow up on his evangelistic and church-planting efforts. Consequently, he launched his third journey traveling throughout "the region of Galatia and Phrygia, *strengthening all the disciples*" (Acts 18:23).

During this third journey, Paul returned to Ephesus as he had promised, and he stayed there for more than two years. He taught "daily in the lecture hall of Tyrannus" (Acts 19:9). People from throughout the region came to this great commercial center to do business and to worship in the temple of Artemis (also called Diana). Many of these pagans were converted to Christianity. As they returned to their hometowns, they shared their experiences with others, who then responded to the gospel as well. As a result, churches were established throughout Asia (see Acts 19:26).

Because of Paul's extended stay in Ephesus, this third journey lasted approximately six years. But rather than return to Antioch and Syria, as he had done following the first two journeys, Paul was determined to go to Jerusalem. It was there he faced tremendous opposition and almost lost his life. But he escaped to Caesarea where he was incarcerated for two years before appealing to the Roman ruler, Caesar. He was then sent on to Rome where he was held for another two years, under house arrest (see Acts 28:30-31 and figure 3.4.)

Beyond the Book of Acts

After Paul's first imprisonment in Rome, he continued his church-planting efforts. Many scholars believe that upon his release he went to Macedonia and Asia, revisiting the churches there. Paul also traveled with Titus to the pagan land of Crete, where they founded more churches. These conclusions are based on geographical references not found in Acts but mentioned in the pastoral epistles of 1 and 2 Timothy and Titus.

A WRITTEN MINISTRY

As we have just seen, Acts outlines the face-to-face and hands-on church-planting ministry of Paul and his companions. However, under the direction of the Holy Spirit, Paul developed a follow-up technique that gives us valuable insights as to how to measure a church. The 13 letters he wrote to these local congregations make up a large section of the New Testament. As we explore the biblical criteria for measuring a church, we will look at these and other letters. We will consider these letters in chronological order, according to the dates they were likely written, not in the order that they appear in the printed New Testament. Appendix C will help place all of these letters in sequence and in the context of the historical record in Acts.

Paul's Prison Epistles

In this chapter, let's look at three letters that Paul wrote during his first imprisonment in Rome: Ephesians, Colossians and Philippians. Each one has a similar focus, which I call a perfect measurement. Paul wanted these churches to reflect the very life of the Lord Jesus Christ![3]

Remember, these letters were written after approximately 12 years of intense church-planting efforts (see appendix D). During that time, Paul had experienced firsthand the ongoing and often very difficult challenges of developing maturity in new believers, many who were converted out of deeply-steeped pagan lifestyles. He had encountered and confronted the issue of balancing law and grace, an issue that often divides churches. He had seen the lingering influences of idolatry and immorality in new converts. Moreover, after returning to Jerusalem, he faced his most difficult challenge with his own people, the Jews. He found it hard to believe that this once dynamic church, described so specifically in the opening chapters of Acts (see Acts 2:42-47), had become permeated with tradition.

As Paul sat chained to a Roman guard in Rome, he wrote these three powerful letters that reflected his own growth and maturity in determining how to measure a church. As we will see, he clearly focused on our becoming like Jesus Christ, not just as individuals but as local bodies of believers. In fact, no one Christian can by himself or herself adequately reflect Jesus Christ. It takes a community of faith—believers who are manifesting the fruit of the Spirit in their relationships with one another (see Gal. 5:22-23).

It is amazing to see how Paul used human and divine creativity to present Jesus Christ as the perfect measurement of a local church. Each section of each letter is expressed in a unique way, but each section focuses clearly on the God-man, the Lord Jesus Christ.

The Whole Measure of the Fullness of Christ

After describing their wonderful calling in Christ in the first three chapters of Ephesians, Paul went on to urge believers "to live a life worthy" of this calling (Eph. 4:1). Describing the Lord's strategy for spiritual growth, he penned the following powerful words:

> It was he who gave some to be apostles, some to be prophets, some to be evangelists, and some to be pastors and teachers, to prepare God's people for works of service, so that the body of Christ may be built up until we all reach unity in the faith and in the knowledge of the

> Son of God and become mature, *attaining to the whole measure of the fullness of Christ* (Eph. 4:11-13).

The term "measure," which Paul used in his letter to the Ephesians, is translated from the Greek word *metron* and refers to God's standard for evaluating and measuring the maturity level of both the universal Church and local assemblies. Local churches are to be the visible expressions of the universal Church. It is also very apparent that the ultimate standard is Jesus Christ Himself, particularly the way He lived during the days He walked on Earth as the incarnate Son of God. Paul wrote that all believers *together* should attain "to the *whole measure* [metron] *of the fullness of Christ*" (Eph. 4:13).

The Incarnate Son of God

Paul defined maturity in a corporate or collective sense. God's plan is that "we *all* come to the unity of the faith and knowledge of the Son of God, *to a perfect man, to the measure of the stature of the fullness of Christ*" (Eph. 4:13, *NKJV*).

In this passage, Paul used the *singular* term "man" to illustrate the *corporate* body of Christ.[4] Furthermore, he described this man as perfect or mature (Greek, *teleios*).

I believe Paul used this phrase "perfect man" as a metaphor to illustrate that all members of Christ's Body are to reflect the *perfect Son of God*, the one who "became flesh and made his dwelling among us" (John 1:14).

Paul used the same metaphor when writing to the Corinthians, reminding them that when he "was a child, . . . [he] talked . . . thought . . . [and] reasoned like a child." However, when he "*became a man*," he "put childish ways behind" him (1 Cor. 13:11). In both instances, Paul was saying that the Church (both universal and local) should become mature, reflecting its founder, Jesus Christ.

Reaching this state of maturity will not happen in an absolute sense until the Church has been caught up and presented to Christ. As the apostle John wrote, "We know that when he [Jesus Christ] appears, *we shall be like him*, for *we shall see him as he is*" (1 John 3:2). In his letter to the Corinthians, Paul describes this moment as being "face-to-face" with Christ (1 Cor. 13:12).

John's Marvelous Vision

As an old man in exile on the Isle of Patmos, John witnessed this glorious, future and eternal moment in a prophetic vision and recorded it in Revelation 19:6-8:

> Then I heard what sounded like a great multitude, like the roar of rushing waters and like loud peals of thunder, shouting:
>
> "Hallelujah!
> For our Lord God Almighty reigns.
> Let us rejoice and be glad
> and give him glory!
> For the wedding of the Lamb
> has come,
> and his bride has made
> herself ready.
> Fine linen, bright and clean,
> was given her to wear."
>
> *(Fine linen stands for the righteous acts of the saints.)*

Believers of All Ages

John actually saw two groups of people in his vision. First, there was the larger group, all of those who were "invited to the wedding supper of the Lamb" (Rev. 19:9). These are the true believers of all ages.

John did not tell us specifically who was in this great multitude. However, all of those mentioned in the Old Testament hall of faith in Hebrews 11 will certainly be shouting these great hallelujahs, including Enoch, Noah, Abraham, Isaac, Jacob, Joseph and Joshua. Of course, most members of their families will likely be standing beside them and lifting their voices in praise to God. In fact, all of those who had been true, believing Israelites will be there—those who through the centuries prior to Christ's first coming had by faith experienced "circumcision of the heart, by the Spirit, not by the written code" (Rom. 2:29; see also Rom. 9:6).

There, however, will also be many God-fearing Gentiles in that great multitude—people such as Rahab the harlot and her family (see Heb. 11:31). When she protected the spies in Jericho, she testified that she was a true believer in the God of Abraham, Isaac and Jacob (see Josh. 2:11). The collective voices in this great multitude will sound like the roar of rushing waters, a virtual Niagara Falls.

The Bride of Christ

Why were these believers of all ages praising God? Because there was a second group present that occupied center stage. The members of this group were not shouting but *listening*, no doubt worshiping in silent humility. In John's vision, he saw the Church, the Body of Christ, being presented to Jesus Christ.

As John described this scene, the Holy Spirit inspired him to select another beautiful metaphor to illustrate the Church: a Bride who had adorned herself for her Bridegroom. Merrill C. Tenney has stated, "The marriage of the Lamb is certainly figurative of the ultimate union of Christ with His people. [Even though] the word 'Church' is not used here, the bride can scarcely mean anything else."[5]

When I think about this metaphor, I often visualize my daughter Robyn's wedding. It was a large celebration attended by nearly 1,000 people. I had the privilege of giving her away. Dressed in a beautiful, spotless, white wedding gown, she made her glorious entrance. What a moving experience!

No earthly wedding will ever be as glorious and magnificent as when God the Father presents His Son, Jesus Christ, to His eternal Bride—the Church.

However, no earthly wedding will ever be as glorious and magnificent as when God the Father presents His Son, Jesus Christ, to His eternal Bride—the Church. We will then be ultimately perfect—measuring up to the fullness of Christ. In that day, all members of the Body of Christ will be given to the Savior "as a radiant church, without stain or wrinkle or any other blemish, but holy and blameless" (Eph. 5:27).

The Church in the World

Although someday "we will all be changed" (1 Cor. 15:51) and we will be with Christ and like Him, until then we must live in the present—just as New Testament Christians lived in their present moment. We have not yet been caught up to meet Jesus face-to-face (see 1 Cor. 13:12). In the meantime, it is God's plan that "each part does its work." We are to grow together as believers, reflecting the righteousness, compassion and love of Jesus Christ more and more each day (see Eph. 4:16). This is why John, in his first epistle, exhorted us in the *here* and *now*: "Everyone who has this hope in him purifies himself, just as he is pure" (1 John 3:3). Although this is a personal exhortation, Paul made it clear in his Ephesian letter that purity is to be a hallmark of the Christian community. As we have seen, we are to become "a radiant church" that is "holy and blameless" (Eph. 5:27).

Eternal and Earthly

The apostle Paul probably had in mind both *eternal* and *earthly* perspectives for the Church when he penned the words "attaining to the whole measure of the fullness of Christ" (Eph. 4:13). But as he continued to describe God's plan for the Church, he focused more specifically on local expressions of the Body of Christ. Consequently, Paul stated that churches in the here and now will mature and become doctrinally stable. Its committed members will not be "infants, tossed back and forth by the waves, and blown here and there by every wind of teaching" (Eph. 4:14). Mature believers know *what* they believe as well as *how* to live. They speak "the truth in love" to one another–and as they do, they "*grow up into him* who is the Head, that is, Christ" (Eph. 4:15). In other words, as a local church grows and matures, its committed core will become more and more like the perfect man, Jesus Christ. *Together,* they will reflect His image. When mature believers live as they should, Christians at various levels of growth, from infants to adolescents, will become a part of the committed and unified core, and together they will display the stature of Jesus Christ.

Treasures of Wisdom and Knowledge

Paul's letter to the Colossians is often called a twin epistle, because it is closely linked to the letter to the Ephesians. However, unlike the Ephesian letter, which was probably written to be read in other churches throughout Asia, the letter to the Colossians was directed to a specific local church. As a result, Paul identified Christians in that city as the "faithful *brothers* [family] in Christ at Colosse" (Col. 1:2).

Although worded differently, the following paragraph from Paul's letter to the Colossians in many respects parallels the paragraph in Ephesians:

> I want you to know how much I am struggling for you and for those at Laodicea, and for all who have not met me personally. My purpose is that they may be encouraged in heart and *united in love,* so that they may have the full riches of complete understanding, *in order that they may know the mystery of God, namely, Christ, in whom are hidden all the treasures of wisdom and knowledge.* I tell you this so that no one may deceive you by fine-sounding arguments. For though I am absent from you in body, I am present with you in spirit and delight to see how orderly you are and how firm your faith in Christ is (2:1-5).

United in Love

Paul's concern for every local church is that all of its members function with one ultimate goal in mind: that "the whole body . . . grows and builds itself up in love" (Eph. 4:16). Jesus prayed for all of us who have come to faith in Christ, that we "may be one" as He was one with the Father (John 17:20-23). Love and unity are interrelated, inseparable concepts. Consequently, Paul wrote to the Colossians to encourage them and the Laodiceans to "be *united* in love" (Col. 2:2).

Complete Understanding

In order to be "united in love" these believers needed to have a "*complete understanding*" of who Jesus really is (Col. 2:2). In other words, in order to attain "the whole measure of the fullness of Christ" (the phrase he used in Ephesians), we must know and understand that in Christ are "hidden all the treasures of wisdom and knowledge" (Col. 2:3). There is no other source of truth, for He *is* the Truth (see John 14:6).

Paul's concern for these believers was the same as his concern for the church in Ephesus and the other churches in Asia—that they as local communities would "reach unity in the faith and in the *knowledge* [that is "the full riches of complete understanding"] *of the Son of God*" (Col. 2:2). Then and only then would they become "mature, attaining to the whole measure of the fullness of Christ" (Eph. 4:13). When this began to happen, they would "no longer be infants, tossed back and forth . . . by *every wind of teaching* and by the *cunning* and *craftiness* of men in their *deceitful scheming*" (Eph. 4:14).

Correct Teaching

Becoming doctrinally stable was a problem in Colosse and Laodicea, just as it was in Ephesus and the churches in Asia. This is why Paul wrote: "I tell you this so no one may deceive you by *fine-sounding arguments*" (Col. 2:4). They needed to know that in Christ are "hidden all the treasures of wisdom and knowledge" (2:3)—truth was not to be found in the wisdom of this world (see 1 Cor. 2:1-5 and Jas. 3:13-18).

The moment we take our eyes off of the Lord Jesus Christ as our model and example, we cease to be the church God intended us to be! We can have no other focus and still be truly Christian—and mature. Paul made this point abundantly clear to the Colossians and Laodiceans who were dabbling in a belief system that Paul categorically called "hollow and deceptive philosophy" because it was based on "human tradition and the basic principles of this world rather than on Christ" (Col. 2:8).

Face-to-Face

Paul also made clear the correlation between our corporate life on this Earth and our corporate life at the rapture, when we will become like Christ in His perfection. "When Christ, who is your life, appears," Paul wrote, "then you also will appear with him in glory" (Col. 3:4). In other words, as John stated, we will "be like him, for we shall see him as he is" (1 John 3:2). At that moment, "we will all be changed—in a flash, in the twinkling of an eye" (1 Cor. 15:51-52). Perfection will have come, and the imperfect will have disappeared (see 1 Cor. 13:10). We will no longer "know in part"; rather, we will "know fully" (1 Cor. 13:12). We will be face-to-face with our Savior, the Lord Jesus Christ.

Paul's concern then for the Colossians and the Laodiceans was the same as his concern for the Ephesians and the other communities of faith in Asia. He wanted them to attain "to the whole measure of the fullness of Christ" (Eph. 4:13).

Having the Attitude of Christ Jesus

As Paul sat chained to a Roman guard, he also wrote to the Philippians—probably during the same year he wrote to the Ephesians and to the Colossians. Once again, he focused on Jesus Christ as the true measure of a church. Becoming even more creative, Paul appealed to the Lord's models of *servanthood, humility* and *sacrifice* that identified with our humanity:

> Your attitude [as a body of believers in Philippi] should be the same as that of *Christ Jesus:* Who, being in very nature God, did not consider equality with God something to be grasped, but made himself nothing, taking the very nature of a *servant,* being made in human like-

> ness. And being found in appearance as a man, he *humbled himself* and became *obedient to death*—even death on a cross! (Phil. 2:5-8).

How are Christ's attitudes of servanthood, humility and sacrifice reflected in the church? First, note that Paul used the second-person plural ("your attitude") to address the believers in Philippi. It is also clear from the context he was addressing their relationships with one another. He was appealing to their corporate attitude, which includes both a corporate endeavor and a corporate result—not just a personal discipline leading to personal maturity. Paul taught the Ephesians that to arrive at this corporate attitude, each part must do its work. Then—and only then—will the local body of Christ be "held together by every supporting ligament" and "build itself up in love," which is reflecting the stature of Jesus Christ.

Second, note that Paul's preface to what is often called the great *kenosis* passage leaves nothing to the imagination in terms of this community endeavor:

1. **Servanthood** enables Christians to be like-minded and to become one in spirit and purpose (see Phil. 2:2).
2. **Humility** eliminates selfish ambition and vain conceit and causes us to consider others better than ourselves (see v. 3).
3. **Sacrifice** enables us not only to look to our "own interests, but also to the interests of others" (v. 4).[6]

In this letter, Paul emphasized the significance of *the stature of Jesus Christ* that should serve as a measurement for a maturing church. When a church community demonstrates these qualities, it is well on its way to "attaining to the whole measure of the fullness of Christ" (Eph. 4:13).

This is why Paul prayed the following prayer for these believers in Philippi:

> And this is my prayer: that *your love* [as a body of believers] may abound more and more in knowledge and depth of insight ["the full riches of complete understanding," (Col. 2:2)], so that *you* [as a community] may be able to discern what is best and may be pure and blameless *until the day of Christ*, filled with the fruit of righteousness that comes *through Jesus Christ*—to the glory and praise of God (Phil. 1:9-11).

Guiding Principles

Principle 1. When measuring a church, we must look for the degree to which believers have a true understanding of who the Lord Jesus Christ really is.

As I was writing this chapter, two articles in the *Dallas Morning News* caught my attention. One featured the well-known Catholic theologian Roger Haight. In his controversial book *Jesus Symbol of God*, he "explores the possibility that non-Christians can get to heaven without the help of Jesus."[7] He argues that Jesus is the path to salvation for Christians, but that for non-Christians, God may work in other ways. Predictably, this point of view has stirred up a lot of tension within Roman Catholic circles, but it represents the new thinking that is engaging the minds of theologians in both Roman Catholic and Protestant circles.

The second article was authored by John Stott, rector emeritus of All Soul's Church in London, England. In his article, Stott cites a Harvard scholar, H. J. Cadbury, who wrote a book titled *The Peril of Modernizing Jesus*. Using this theme as a starting point, Stott then warned that in this new millennium, "We need to go back to the authentic Jesus of the New Testament witness, whether this Jesus is acceptable to modern people or not."[8] In other words, "there is but [only] one Lord, Jesus Christ" (1 Cor. 8:6).

Stott is right! We must not compromise the biblical doctrine of Christology. If we do, we compromise the very essence and heart of Christianity, which would be tantamount to theological suicide.

However, on the pragmatic side, Stott goes on to raise a very important question that we all need to think about:

> How can we be loyal to the authentic Jesus and simultaneously present Him relevantly to our contemporaries?[9]

Once again, I agree with Stott's answer:

> It is good to present Jesus in the best possible light, so as to commend Him to the world. But it is not good, in order to do so, to eliminate from the portrait everything which might offend, including the offense of the cross.[10]

Principle 2. When measuring a church, we must evaluate the degree to which believers reflect the life and glory of the Lord Jesus Christ.

No Christian alone can achieve this goal. It is true, of course, that as individual believers, we are to become like Christ. This was certainly Paul's instructional goal when he wrote to the Colossians, "We proclaim him, admonishing and teaching *everyone* with all wisdom, so that we may present *everyone* perfect in Christ" (Col. 1:28). However, Paul also taught that the only way to achieve this goal is in the context of community, which is of divine design. He made this clear when he stated that his desire for both the Colossians and the Laodiceans was that they be "united in love" (Col. 2:2).

THINKING AND GROWING TOGETHER

1. What is a biblical view of who Jesus Christ really is?
2. Why will false views of who Jesus is lead to a church that will never measure up to God's standards as outlined in Scripture?
3. What are some of the false views of Christ? Why are they false?
4. Why do some churches have a true view of who Jesus Christ really is, yet not measure up to the biblical standard of maturity described by Paul in his prison epistles?

Notes

1. Rick Warren, *The Purpose-Driven Church* (Grand Rapids, MI: Zondervan, 1995).
2. Robert Lewis with Rob Wilkins, *The Church of Irresistible Influence* (Grand Rapids, MI: Zondervan, 2001).
3. Most conservative scholars believe that Paul wrote Ephesians, Colossians, Philippians and Philemon during his first imprisonment in Rome. Furthermore, he probably wrote all of them in the same year, A.D. 61.
4. Though the translators of the *NIV* omit the specific word, it is clearly used in the Greek text as translated in the *NKJV*. As stated by A. Skevington Wood, "The phrase is literally 'into a perfect, full-grown man' (*eis andra teleion*)." *The Expositors Bible Commentary*, vol. 11, (Grand Rapids, MI: Zondervan, 1978), p. 59.
5. Merrill C. Tenney, *Interpreting Revelation* (Grand Rapids, MI: Wm. B. Eerdmans Publishing Co., 1957), p. 87.

6. In this passage, Paul used the Greek word "*ekenosen*" that relates to the way Christ emptied Himself. This concept gave birth to what has been called *kenosis* theories, or ideas regarding what actually happened when "the Word became flesh and made his dwelling among us" (John 1:14).
7. Michael Paulson, "Thinker Under Fire: Theologian Disciplined for Views on Jesus, Salvation of Non-Christians," *Dallas Morning News*, April 28, 2001, p. 4G.
8. John R. W. Stott, "Which Jesus Are We Talking About Now?" *Dallas Morning News*, March 17, 2001, p. 4G.
9. Ibid.
10. Ibid.

CHAPTER 4

REFLECTING GOD'S GRACE

This is an intensely personal chapter for me. I grew up in a church where grace, particularly as it related to salvation, was virtually an unspoken word. Whenever it was used, very few people really knew what it meant, including me.

Fortunately, my parents, although long-time members of this church, had been listening to Christian radio and learned that salvation was a free gift. Hence, through their influence I accepted the Lord Jesus Christ as my Savior at age 16 and I also became a member of this church.

However, there was a very important missing ingredient in my understanding of grace. Though I believed I was saved by grace through faith—which the majority in this church did *not* understand—I still believed I kept myself saved by *doing* certain things. If I slipped up and fell short of God's standards, which I later discovered were the standards of this particular church rather than of God, I became fearful that I might lose my eternal relationship with my creator. Needless to say, my spiritual and emotional life was an often chaotic, roller-coaster experience. I often felt depressed and defeated in my Christian life.

Sadly, what I have just shared about my personal experience illustrates the corporate life of the whole church I grew up in—and other churches in that denomination. In fact, if you asked individual members whether or not they knew for sure that they were saved and had eternal life, most of them would say they never had an assurance of their salvation. They could only wait and see! If they obeyed the "rules of the church," they might have a chance to enter heaven. Even though I was a young believer and still confused about the biblical concept of grace, I knew something was desperately wrong with this scene.

Amazing Grace

We all want to understand grace, but what is it and how does it relate to our salvation experiences and the way we live our Christian lives? I am not alone in my perplexity. This is obvious when we look at the subjects of some of the books that became best-sellers around the turn of the millennium. For example, respected author Philip Yancey addressed this issue in his own life in his landmark book *What's So Amazing About Grace?* He had belonged to a church in which the people were taught about "the dispensation of grace" but were also presented with a set of rules that resembled what he called "the dispensation of law." Yancey grew up "with the strong impression that a person becomes spiritual by attending to the gray-area rules." He contends that his fellow church members had their "own pecking order rivaling the Orthodox Jews."[1]

Fortunately, Yancey did not give up on the Church. Although he may appear to be a bit caustic at times, he now writes out of a deep concern, hoping the Church comes to understand and reflect the biblical concept of grace. He explains:

> As I look back on my own pilgrimage, marked by my wanderings, detours, and dead-ends, I see now that what pulled me along was my search for grace. I rejected the church for a time because I found so little grace there. I returned because I found grace nowhere else.[2]

This is a profound conclusion. What Yancey is declaring is that in his own search he discovered no other religious or social system that offers the wonderful message of grace that is described in the Bible. I believe his search could have gone on forever and he still would have come up with the same conclusion. The Church as God designed it is the only place grace can be demonstrated. When rightly understood and practiced, this wonderful reflection is a powerful mark of corporate maturity. In other words, a church that does not demonstrate true grace as God intended is not a mature church. *Grace is truly an amazing concept!*

Andrew H. Trotter declares that "the word *grace* in biblical terms can, like forgiveness, repentance, regeneration and salvation mean something as broad as describing the whole of God's activity towards man or as narrow as describing one segment of that activity." He goes on to conclude that an "accurate common definition describes grace as the unmerited favor of God towards men."[3]

A Great Salvation

As Trotter implies, New Testament writers used the Greek term "*charis*" to describe "the whole of God's activity" in relating to mankind. Of the many ways this word is utilized, none is more profound, meaningful and freeing than when grace is used to describe the way Christians are saved. The author of Hebrews calls this marvelous experience "a great salvation" (Heb. 2:3). The most succinct declaration and explanation of grace appears in Paul's letter to the Ephesians:

> For it is by grace you have been saved, through faith—and this not from yourselves, it is the gift of God—not by works, so that no one can boast (2:8-9).

Unfortunately, many Church leaders today have added a works formula to God's grace in saving us. But this is not a new problem. It has existed throughout Church history.

The Churches in Galatia

Paul faced this theological confusion, particularly in the early days of his ministry. When establishing churches in Pisidian Antioch, Lystra, Iconium and Derbe, Jewish teachers came into these churches after Paul and Barnabas had left and taught the believers that they could not be saved by grace alone.

This is not surprising since there were significant Jewish settlements located outside Jerusalem, particularly in Pisidian Antioch and Iconium. When Paul and Barnabas arrived in these cities, they entered the Jewish synagogues first, waited for an invitation to speak and then shared the good news regarding Jesus Christ (see Acts 13:14-15). When both Jewish people and Gentiles responded to the gospel, it engendered jealousy and hostility, particularly among the Jewish inhabitants of these cities. The resistance became so intense that Paul and Barnabas had to move from city to city (see Acts 13:45-52;14:1-7,19-20).

This missionary team eventually returned to these major cities, "strengthening the disciples and encouraging them to remain true to the faith" (Acts 14:22). They even appointed elders in each church to shepherd these new believers (see Acts 14:20-23). However, Jewish religious leaders began a counter-movement after Paul and Barnabas left. These teachers insisted that no one could be saved without keeping Jewish customs, particularly the rite of circumcision.

A Distressing Report

After returning to his "sending" church in Antioch in Syria (see figure 3.1), Paul evidently received a distressing report regarding this theological confusion. He wasted no time in penning a letter to the churches in Galatia and addressed the issue head-on:

> You foolish Galatians! Who has bewitched you? Before your very eyes Jesus Christ was clearly portrayed as crucified. I would like to learn just one thing from you: Did you receive the Spirit by observing the law, or by *believing* what you heard? Are you so foolish? After beginning with the Spirit, are you now trying to attain your goal by *human effort?* (Gal. 3:1-3).

Paul went on to cite Abraham's experience, reminding these first-century believers that this Old Testament patriarch "*believed* God, and it was *credited to him as righteousness*" (Gal. 3:6). In other words, salvation was based on faith alone, even during the Old Testament era. Furthermore, Abraham was able to put his faith in God because of God's unmerited favor. Apart from grace, he could not have believed!

In the same way, Paul continued, "those who *believe* are children of Abraham" (Gal. 3:7). Making this point even more emphatic, Paul declared unequivocally that "no one is justified before God by the law, because, 'The righteous will live by faith'" (Gal. 3:11).

The Church in Rome

Paul expanded upon this truth when he wrote to believers in Rome. He asked them under what circumstances Abraham's "faith was credited to him as righteousness" (Rom. 4:9). In other words, when was Abraham saved, before or after he was circumcised? Without any element of uncertainty, Paul answered his own question. Abraham was saved *before* he was circumcised (see Rom. 4:10). "So then," Paul wrote, "[Abraham] is the father of *all who believe,*" the Jews who have been circumcised and those Gentiles who have not! (Rom. 4:11).

Paul culminated this section of his letter with one of the greatest conclusions in all of Scripture:

> Therefore, since we have been *justified through faith* [just like Abraham], we have peace with God through our Lord Jesus Christ, through whom we have gained *access by faith into this grace* in which we now stand. And we rejoice in the hope of the glory of God (Rom. 5:1-2).

A Personal Turning Point

After I became a Christian and joined the church, I decided to attend Moody Bible Institute in Chicago. However, when I began my studies, I was not prepared for the spiritual and emotional turmoil I would feel as I explored the Scriptures. Although I had *become* a Christian when I put my faith in Jesus Christ, I still believed I *kept* myself saved by doing good works. Early in my formal studies, my church traditions became a stumbling block and blurred my thinking. I had difficulty understanding what the Bible (*sola scriptura*) said about grace. Perhaps more accurately, I struggled to accept what the Bible so clearly taught about grace: My salvation was based on faith alone (*sola fide*).

One day, as I was meditating on the book of Romans, I came face-to-face with the questions Paul raised about Abraham. How was he saved? Clearly, it was before he was circumcised. In fact, it was long before God gave Moses the Law at Mount Sinai. The answer to Paul's question penetrated my heart. For the first time in my Christian experience, I realized that I was not only saved by grace but also kept by God's grace (*sola gratia*). Suddenly, I also understood the answer to Paul's questions in Romans 8:

- If God is for us, who can be against us? (v. 31).
- Who will bring any charge against those whom God has chosen? (v. 33).
- Who shall separate us from the love of Christ? (v. 35).

Instantly I understood and believed that I was not only justified (made righteous) by faith in Jesus Christ, but also, in God's sight, I was already *glorified!* (see Rom. 8:30). Nothing could separate me from God's love—not even my own doubts and failures! Paul's final words in Romans 8 gripped my soul. His personal testimony from his heart came true in my own heart:

> For I am convinced that neither death nor life, neither angels nor demons, neither the present nor the future, nor any powers, neither height nor depth, nor anything else in all creation, will be able to separate us from the love of God that is in Christ Jesus our Lord (vv. 38-39).

From that moment forward I had a new sense of inner peace. I finally had the assurance of my salvation. The ambivalence I had often felt dissipated. Though I went through my normal emotional ups and downs, my psychological status did not affect my sense of security and hope in Jesus Christ. I did not feel saved one day and lost the next. Every day I knew that I was saved.

What About Works?

Though this was a life-changing experience, I still struggled with an argument that is often posed by Christians who believe they can lose their salvation. In fact, before my encounter with Paul's message in Romans, I had often used this argument myself when debating with other students at Moody Bible Institute. If we believe and teach that we are eternally saved and that nothing can separate us from God, then what keeps Christians from living any way they want to live?

Paul anticipated this same argument as he penned his letter to the Romans. Lifting questions out of the minds of those people who may believe that the doctrine of eternal salvation will lead to license, he wrote:

> What shall we say, then? Shall we go on sinning that grace may increase? (Rom. 6:1).

Paul answered these questions with two emphatic statements and another question:

> By no means! We died to sin; how can we live in it any longer? (Rom. 6:2).

Frankly, I struggled with this issue for a period of time, even after I experienced the assurance of my salvation. After all, if

Christians are not threatened with the possibility of losing their salvation, then how can they be motivated to live godly and righteous lives?

Disciplined by Grace

Several months after graduating from Moody, I had another unique experience that also became life changing and had a huge impact on my ministry as a pastor. A friend gave me a copy of John Strombeck's book *Disciplined by Grace*.[4] I soon discovered that this volume is a classic exposition of Paul's powerful and penetrating words to Titus, who had stayed in Crete to establish the churches which he and Paul had planted. Titus wrote:

> For the *grace of God that brings salvation* has appeared to all men. *It teaches us* to say "No" to *ungodliness* and *worldly passions,* and to live *self-controlled, upright* and *godly lives* in this present age, while we wait for the blessed hope—the glorious appearing of our great God and Savior, Jesus Christ, who gave himself for us to redeem us from *all wickedness* and *to purify* for himself a people that are his very own, *eager to do what is good* (Titus 2:11-14).

Paul made it clear that once we are saved by grace, it is that same grace that teaches us how to live in the will of God. In essence, this is the second part of Paul's statement to the Ephesians in chapter 2. We are indeed saved by grace through faith and not by works (see Eph. 2:8-9)—but we are also *"God's workmanship*, created in Christ Jesus *to do good works,* which God prepared in advance for us to do" (Eph. 2:10).

Truth That Leads to Godliness

Paul made it clear that if we are going to be taught by God's grace, then we need very specific instructions regarding how to live "self-controlled, upright and godly lives" (Titus 2:12). We need someone to teach us the content of this grace. Thus Paul exhorted Titus to "encourage and rebuke with all authority" (Titus 2:15) and to teach with deep conviction and passion those qualities of life that are "in accord with sound doctrine" (Titus 2:1). This is why he outlined in detail how "older men" (Titus 2:2), "younger men" (Titus 2:6), "older women" (Titus 2:3), "younger women" (Titus 2:4) and believing servants (see Titus 2:9-10) are to live in the light of God's marvelous grace in electing, calling and saving us. In fact, Paul began this letter to Titus by saying that it is "knowledge of the truth that leads to godliness" (Titus 1:1).

Godly living, then, does not come automatically, even though we are "God's workmanship, created in Christ Jesus to do good works" (Eph. 2:10). If these good works were a guaranteed result of salvation, all believers would be living godly lives. But those who are converted out of a pagan lifestyle often have no knowledge of the will of God. Consequently, they must be taught very specifically what Christlike qualities they should exemplify in their relationships with God and other people.

God's Mercy

To achieve this goal, Paul took a twofold approach that is beautifully illustrated in his letter to the Romans. He devoted more than half of the letter (the first 11 chapters) to explaining God's grace and mercy in saving us. He then used the rest of the letter to teach us how to live in view of what God has done for us (see Rom. 12-16). This, of course, is succinctly summarized in Paul's transitional statements in the opening verses of Romans 12:

> Therefore, I urge you, brothers, in view of *God's mercy* [all that Paul had written about God's grace in Romans 1-11], to offer your bodies as living sacrifices, holy and pleasing

> to God—this is your spiritual act of worship. Do not conform any longer to the pattern of this world, but be transformed by the renewing of your mind. Then you will be able to test and approve what God's will is—his good, pleasing and perfect will [which Paul then outlined in chapters 12-16] (vv. 1-2).

Our Ultimate Motivation

Paul appealed to these believers in Rome—and to us in the twenty-first century—to live in the will of God and to base our faith on God's mercy toward us. This should be the ultimate motivation for living godly lives. In other words, once we really comprehend the grace that God has bestowed on us and the price Jesus Christ paid to redeem us from sin, how can we do less than present our bodies as living sacrifices? How can we deliberately continue to sin and take advantage of God's grace? This is in essence what Paul asked in Romans 6 and then answered with a resounding No! We cannot! We must not! This would be the ultimate act of ingratitude.

Paul's Apostolic Calling

Paul clearly recognized that it was also through God's unmerited favor (grace) that he became the apostle to the Gentiles. In fact, he had difficulty accepting God's mercy in not only saving him, but also in calling him to preach the very gospel he tried to destroy. Writing to the Corinthians, he humbly declared:

> For I am the least of the apostles and do not even deserve to be called an apostle, because I have persecuted the church of God. But by the grace of God [God's unmerited favor] I am what I am (1 Cor. 15:9-10).[5]

The Grace Gifts

There is also a direct correlation between the gifts of the Spirit and God's grace. God sovereignly chose to give New Testament believers spiritual gifts, particularly to verify the gospel message that Christ died and rose again. For example, Luke recorded the following:

> With great power the apostles continued to testify to the resurrection of the Lord Jesus, and *much grace was upon them all* (Acts 4:33).

Paul continued the same theme when he wrote to the Romans:

> We have different *gifts,* according to the *grace given us* (Rom. 12:6).

We must remember, however, that God gave these gifts freely and according to *His will.*[6] They were given because of a choice God made, which is why the word "*grace*" was used to describe these gifts. They came because of God's unmerited favor. This was also why the author of Hebrews wrote:

> How shall we escape if we ignore such a great salvation? This salvation, which was first announced by the Lord, was confirmed to us by those who heard him. God also testified to it [this salvation] by signs, wonders and various miracles, and *gifts of the Holy Spirit distributed according to His will* (2:3-4).

A Divine Source of Strength

New Testament writers also used the word "grace" to describe a divine source of strength and power that enabled them to live victorious lives in Jesus Christ, regardless of circumstances. For example, when Paul asked the Lord to remove his thorn in the flesh, which is never defined with specifics, the Lord responded:

> My *grace* is sufficient for you, for my *power* is made perfect in weakness (2 Cor. 12:9).

As Paul faced death in a Roman dungeon, he penned his final letter, which was written to Timothy:

> You then, my son, *be strong in the grace* that is in Christ Jesus (2 Tim. 2:1).

The author of Hebrews also referred to grace as a source of strength, especially during times of temptation and weakness. Since Jesus Christ has been tempted in every way, just as we are, as our great high priest, He is able to sympathize with our struggles. Therefore, we are encouraged to seek the Lord's help. We read:

> Let us then approach the *throne of grace* with confidence, so that we may *receive mercy* and *find grace* to help us in our time of need (Heb. 4:16).

> It is good for our hearts to be *strengthened by grace* (Heb. 13:9).

Note the significant difference between the specific grace gifts and the abundant grace that God promises to strengthen all of us in our Christian living. On the one hand, God supernaturally bestows specific grace gifts at His discretion (see Eph. 4:11). On the other hand, the grace to help all believers in times of need is always available through the throne of grace. We are encouraged *to pray* for this sustaining grace to strengthen us and our fellow believers.

A Powerful Greeting and Benediction

The apostle Paul used the Greek work "*charis*" (grace) along with the Hebrew sentiment of "*shalom*" (peace) to greet believers. In fact, he penned these greetings in all 13 of his letters. But when he closed each letter, he focused only on the word "grace." Again and again, he pronounced the following benediction with minor variations: "The *grace* of our Lord Jesus Christ be with you."[7] This pattern is significant! When Paul concluded each of his letters, he was in essence praying that these New Testament believers would experience God's grace as a divine source of strength in their lives.

This was not just a Pauline approach, which further demonstrates the significance of this pattern. Peter and John often expressed the same greeting in the opening section of their letters and concluded by offering a final prayer for grace. In fact, John ends the book of Revelation, which was written to the seven churches, with this same benediction: "The *grace* of the Lord Jesus Christ be with God's people. Amen" (Rev. 22:21).[8]

Generosity

When Paul wrote to the Corinthians, he used the word "grace" to describe generosity with material possessions. This is a very specific way we can draw upon God's strength. His grace is available to help us to "seek first" the Lord's "kingdom and his righteousness"—trusting God that all things we need will be given us as well (Matt. 6:33). Writing to the Corinthians, Paul exhorted, "But just as you excel in everything—in faith, in speech, in knowledge, in complete earnestness and in your love for us—see that you also excel in this grace of giving" (2 Cor. 8:7). In fact, Paul actually used the Greek word *charis* to refer to the "money," or "offering," he had received from various churches to be distributed to others in need (see 2 Cor. 8:19).[9]

Giving Thanks

Many times the authors of Scripture use the word "grace" as a synonym for "giving thanks." In fact, in these instances, the word "*charis*" is translated in this way. For example, Paul wrote to the Corinthians and declared: "But thanks be to God! He gives us the victory through our Lord Jesus Christ" (1 Cor. 15:57).

What an appropriate way to end our study on grace! God has bestowed His unmerited favor on us, both in providing for our salvation and in providing us with the resources to live in the will of God. Can we do less than say thanks?

Paul captured this sentiment in his letter to the Colossians:

> Let the peace of Christ rule in your hearts, since as members of one body you were called to peace. And be *thankful.* Let the word of Christ dwell in you richly as you teach and admonish one another with all wisdom, and as you sings psalms, hymns and spiritual songs with *gratitude* [grace; thanksgiving] in your hearts to God. And whatever you do, whether in word or deed, do it all in the name of the Lord Jesus, giving thanks to God the Father through him (3:15-17).[10]

Guiding Principles

Principle 1. When measuring a church, we must determine the degree to which God's people understand that salvation

is a free gift that results from God's grace—a gift that cannot be earned and that is eternal.

As we have discovered, the most foundational meaning of grace is "God's unmerited favor toward humankind in salvation." When we are justified and saved, it is of God and "no one can say, 'Jesus is Lord,' except by the Holy Spirit" (1 Cor. 12:3).

Millard J. Erickson wrote this truth succinctly, clearly and beautifully:

> Justification is something completely undeserved. It is not an achievement. It is an obtainment, not an attainment. Even faith is not good work, which God must reward with salvation. It is God's gift. It is not the cause of our salvation, but the means by which we receive it. And contrary to the thinking of some, it has always been the means of salvation.[11]

Mature believers are not we-hope-so Christians. Rather, they are we-know-so Christians!

Principle 2. When measuring a church, we must determine the degree to which God's people are motivated to live righteous and holy lives because they clearly understand and deeply appreciate God's grace in having saved them.

A true understanding of God's grace in salvation, on the one hand, keeps the church from becoming legalistic and on the other hand, keeps that same church from practicing license, that is, taking advantage of God's love and mercy.

Churches that practice legalism usually develop a set of rules that are extra-biblical. These rules often grow out of certain cultural situations and focus on external actions, which often leads to hypocrisy. Legalists, in their efforts to behave rightly, often overlook the internal qualities valued by God, such as the fruit of the Spirit (see Gal. 5:22-23). For example, in the church I grew up in, people frequently demonstrated prejudice and judgmental attitudes toward other people who claimed to be Christians but did not belong to the same denomination.

Jesus dealt with this type of religious attitude when He confronted the Pharisees. They had set up legalistic rules within Judaism. However, Jesus called them "hypocrites" and "blind guides." He accused them of straining "out a gnat" but swallowing "a camel" (Matt. 23:23-24).

The Peril of the Pendulum

Legalism in the church is not a true reflection of spiritual maturity. On the other hand, some churches overreact to strictly enforced rules and move toward license. They tend to take liberties in their Christian lives that clearly violate the teachings of Scripture. In other words, people put their faith in Jesus Christ to gain salvation and then, knowing they have God's grace, live sinful lives. This kind of lifestyle–just as legalism–does not reflect true spiritual maturity. A mature church does not reflect either of these extreme positions.

Perfectionism

Some Christians believe that they can become totally like Christ in this life. Unfortunately, when they fail to measure up to His standard, they often suffer intense guilt. Yet all Christians *do* fail! This is why the New Testament letters repeatedly exhort Christians to renew their minds and to be transformed into Christ's image (see Rom. 12:2). This was Paul's goal, too. He knew that he had not "been made perfect" (Phil. 3:12).

Sadly, some Christians who take a perfectionist approach to the Christian life simply give up when they continue to sin. They believe they have failed God and thus have no real hope. Others also believe they have committed the unpardonable sin–what a tragic conclusion to reach! When this happens, certain members in the church may become judgmental and uncaring, which can drive the disillusioned Christian into even greater despair.

I had a close friend in high school who became a Christian at approximately the same time I did. She believed that all Christians can have an experience with God that enables them to reach a level of holiness that actually keeps them from failing God. This, too, is a form of perfectionism. Sadly, my friend had a moral failure.

I remember talking with her one day only to discover that she believed God had given up on her because of her sin. She had lost hope. Nothing I could say seemed to help her understand that God had not forsaken her. Rather, she had forsaken Him and did not believe God would forgive her. I reminded her what happened to the prodigal son, but she had lost hope and not even that story could reach her. The great truth the apostle John outlined for us in his first epistle regarding forgiveness totally eluded her (see 1 John 1:9). How sad. But how encouraging to know that the blood of Jesus Christ continues to cleanse us from all of our sins, including the ones we commit as Christians. If His blood did not cover us, no one could be saved!

Principle 3. When measuring a church, we must determine the degree to which God's people have a correct view of God's holiness.

This principle introduces us to the concept of true worship, which is developed more in-depth in chapter 10. At this point, it is sufficient to understand that Christians who truly comprehend and appreciate God's grace and mercy in saving them will present their bodies to Jesus Christ as "living sacrifices, holy and pleasing to God." Paul calls this a "spiritual act of worship" (Rom. 12:1). But this kind of worship is not only based on what God has done for us but also on who He is! Because He is holy, a mature church should reflect God's holiness (see 1 Pet. 1:16).

This does not mean that we should become perfectionists. Rather, it suggests that through the renewing of our minds, each day we are transformed more and more into the image of Christ. We become more like Jesus in all of our relationships.

Principle 4. When measuring a church, we must determine the degree to which God's people understand God's loving discipline.

Since we are God's children and He is our Father, He will never disown us. However, He *will* discipline us if we constantly disobey Him. He does this because His purpose is always to produce "a harvest of righteousness" in our lives (Heb. 12:7-11).

Since we are God's children and He is our Father, He will never disown us. However, He will *discipline us if we constantly disobey Him.*

The small but power-packed New Testament letters to the seven churches in Asia describe the Lord's discipline of specific churches. For example, John reported the words of Jesus to the church in Ephesus. The Lord commended these believers for certain things, but then went on to state His concerns:

> Yet I hold this against you [all of you]: *You have forsaken your first love.* Remember the height from which you have fallen! Repent and do the things you did at first. *If you do*

not repent, I will come to you and remove your lampstand from its place (Rev. 2:4-5).

There are various opinions regarding what Jesus meant when He said He would remove a church's lampstand. However, we know that the lampstand represented a church—in this instance, the church in Ephesus (see Rev. 1:20). Personally, I believe that God may at times remove His blessing from a church that consistently violates His will. This can happen when the people, in general, or the leadership, in particular, know the truth, but ignore it over a period of time. They continue sinning and do not repent.

We must remember that God's grace also reflects patience, both toward believers and unbelievers (see 2 Pet. 3:8-9). But when a church is consistently unrepentant, it seems that God may discipline that local body by allowing it to actually become ineffective or even nonexistent. In fact, I know of a church in which several in the leadership violated the will of God in their relationship to the pastor. They knowingly and deliberately falsely accused him! Ultimately, because of their behavior, the church split and many of the sheep were scattered; some became so disillusioned they continued to falter in their faith. Unfortunately, years went by before the church acknowledged the sin. Even at this writing, under godly leadership, the church still struggles. Is this a result of God's discipline? Only eternity will tell. But it is a lesson for us all, particularly for us as church leaders.

Principle 5. When measuring a church, we must determine the degree to which God's people are extending grace to one another.

Paul addressed this reflection of grace in his letter to the Romans when he exhorted:

> Accept one another, then, just as Christ accepted you (Rom. 15:7).
>
> Accept him whose faith is weak, without passing judgment on disputable matters (Rom. 14:1).
>
> Therefore let us stop passing judgment on one another. Instead, make up your mind not to put any stumbling block or obstacle in your brother's way (Rom. 14:13).

The context for these and other exhortations conveys Paul's concern regarding judgmental attitudes in the church.

The "disputable matters" in this church involved eating certain kinds of food (see Rom. 14:1) and considering certain days more sacred than others (see Rom. 14:5). Today, churches have their own set of disputable matters that are not spelled out in Scripture as being either good or bad. Often these issues lead to judgmental attitudes and a legalistic environment.

What is the solution? It is twofold. First, Paul exhorted all believers to accept each other just as Christ had accepted them (see Rom. 15:7). Think for a moment what this means! Jesus accepts us just as we are—regardless of our sins, our ethnic backgrounds, our skin color, our economic situation, our political views, our educational background or any other criteria men often use to judge each other. He demonstrates *pure grace* toward us. He demands nothing in response but faith, which He also made possible by His grace. Paul then went on to make the point: "Accept one another, then, just as Christ accepted you" (Rom. 15:7).

However, in many of his letters Paul made it very clear he was not condoning sinful attitudes and actions in the church. Consequently, he gave New Testament believers the other side of love, the tough side. We are to instruct (literally to "admonish") one another when we walk out of the will of God.

However, note the criteria Paul lays out for admonishment of others. What makes us competent to carry out this sensitive task? First, we are to be full of goodness ourselves. This does not mean we must be perfect. None of us could admonish anyone else if that were the standard, not even parents with their children. Instead, it means we must remove the "plank" from our own eye so that "we will see clearly to remove the speck from" our "brother's eye" (Matt. 7:1-5). In other words, we must have our own act together spiritually before we are qualified to help someone else. Paul made it clear that having a judgmental attitude does not qualify us to admonish others.

Second, to carry out this process of admonishment, we are to be complete in knowledge. In other words, we are to deal only with the *specific sins* that are outlined in the Word of God and not those we conjure up.

Principle 6. When measuring a church, we must determine the degree to which God's people are drawing on God's grace to carry out His divine directives.

Thankfully, God's throne of grace is always available to His children. In fact, He has promised us that when we approach this throne through His Son, we will "receive mercy and find grace to help us in our time of need" (Heb. 4:16).

This, I believe, is a primary reason why Paul and the other New Testament authors ended their letters to New Testament Christians with the wonderful benediction, "The grace of our Lord Jesus Christ be with you." Grace is a divine resource that comes from God the Father, Jesus Christ the Son and the blessed Holy Spirit. It is available for the asking! A mature church, therefore, is a praying church. The people of a mature church consistently pray for grace to serve one another in love!

THINKING AND GROWING TOGETHER

1. How do the majority of people in your church interpret Ephesians 2:8-10?
2. What motivates the people in your church to live godly lives? How would the majority interpret Titus 2:11-14?
3. To what extent are the people in your church living out Paul's instructions in Romans 12:1-2?
4. To what extent are the people in your church obeying Paul's exhortations in Romans 15:7 and Romans 15:14?
5. To what extent are the people in your church practicing Hebrews 4:16?

Notes:

1. Philip Yancey, *What's So Amazing About Grace* (Grand Rapids, MI: Zondervan Publishing House, 1997), p. 30.
2. Ibid., p. 16. For other books that express similar sentiments; see Michael Horton, *Putting Amazing Back into Grace* (Grand Rapids, MI: Baker Books, 1994) pp. 21-22; Chuck Swindoll, *The Grace Awakening* (Dallas: Word Publishing, 1996) p. XVIII.
3. Andrew H. Trotter, Jr., "Grace," *Evangelical Dictionary of Biblical Theology*, ed. Walter A. Elwell (Grand Rapids, MI: Baker Books, 1996), p. 312.
4. John Strombeck, *Disciplined by Grace* (Grand Rapids, MI: Kregel Publications, 1991), n.p.
5. For additional information about the relationship between God's grace and Paul's apostolic calling to minister to the Gentiles see Galatians 1:15-16; 2:9-10; 1 Corinthians 3:10; Romans 1:5; 15:15-16; Ephesians 3:2-3,6.
6. For additional information about the relationship between God's grace and the gifts of the Spirit see Acts 2:33; 2:43; 11:23; 1 Corinthians 1:4-7; Ephesians 4:7-8; 1 Peter 4:10.
7. To find this pattern in Scripture see Galatians 6:16; 1 Thessalonians 5:28; 2 Thessalonians 3:18; 1 Corinthians 1:3; 2 Corinthians 13:11; Romans 16:20; Ephesians 6:24; Colossians 4:18; Philippians 4:23; Philemon 25;

1 Timothy 6:21; Titus 3:15; 2 Timothy 4:22.

8. To note this pattern in the non-Pauline letters, see Revelation 22:21; 1 Peter 1:2; 5:14; 2 Peter 1:2; 3:18; 2 John 3; Revelation 1:4.
9. For additional information about the relationship between grace and giving, see 2 Corinthians 8:1,4,6,19; 9:8,14.
10. Where do we get the phrase "Would you say grace?" which we often use before meals? Look up the following references: 1 Corinthians 10:30; 2 Corinthians 2:14; 8:16; 9:15; Romans 6:17; 1 Timothy 1:12; 2 Timothy 1:2; 1 Peter 2:19-20.
11. Millard J. Erickson, *Christian Theology* (Grand Rapids, MI: Baker Book House, 1983), p. 959.

C H A P T E R 5

A DIVINE TRILOGY

Although "attaining to the whole measure of the fullness of Christ" (Eph. 4:13) is the ultimate measure of maturity in a local body of Christians, New Testament writers became even more creative and specific in describing this measurement. Paul particularly, but not exclusively, referred to the manifestation of *faith, hope* and *love*. In fact, this divine trilogy jumps off the pages of the New Testament letters and forms a comprehensive perspective for evaluating corporate Christian living. According to Gordon Fee, "These words embrace the whole of Christian existence, as believers live out the life of the Spirit in the present age, awaiting the consummation."[1] And C. K. Barrett refers to faith, hope and love as "the central, essential and indefectible elements in Christianity."[2]

A few years ago, when we built our worship center at Fellowship Bible Church North, I preached a message on this divine trilogy. A married couple in our church who are skilled in designing and creating stained-glass windows prepared a beautiful window featuring "faith, hope and love" as the true measure of a church. It is located in the front and center of the sanctuary, above the platform from which I preached that very sermon. During our services, I often sit in the front row of the worship center and look up at these three inspiring windows and contemplate the amazing concepts they depict. They always remind me of the ultimate goal for our church—and every church—that God outlined so clearly in Scripture: to become like Jesus Christ.

Paul's Letters

Since Paul wrote more epistles than any other first-century church planter, it is not surprising that we have an abundance of information about the way he used this divine trilogy to measure maturity. In fact, how he applied these words gives us helpful insights into the spiritual status of particular New Testament churches.

The Corinthian Correspondence

To grasp Paul's view of faith, hope and love, let's look first at one of the most immature and worldly churches in the New Testament: the church at Corinth. Its members were so lacking in judgment that Paul told them in no uncertain terms that the way they lived their lives was virtually indistinguishable from the lifestyle of their pagan counterparts. They "were acting like *mere men*," a definite reference to unsaved Corinthians (1 Cor. 3:3). W. Harold Mare reminds us that "to walk *kata anthropon* . . . means to live only the way the ordinary sinful man lives—in selfishness, pride and envy."[3]

Even though Paul had spent a year and a half founding and establishing this church, four or five years later, when he wrote his first letter, he still identified the Christians at Corinth as worldly Christians. After all that time, they were still "infants in Christ" (1 Cor. 3:1-3). They certainly did not measure up to the fullness of Christ, Paul's goal for every local church. The fruit of the Holy Spirit in their lives was woefully missing!

Despite their carnality, most of these Corinthians were true believers. Paul addressed them as *saints* and as "those *sanctified* in Christ Jesus and called to be holy" (1 Cor. 1:2). He repeatedly appealed to them as *brothers* (see appendix B). He identified them as *God's temple* (see 1 Cor. 3:16-17) and as the *Body of Christ* (see 1 Cor. 12:27). They were definitely "in Christ," since Paul used the phrase several times to identify their relationship with God the Father (see 1 Cor. 1:2,30; 3:1; 4:15). They were clearly *saved* by grace and through faith, but as yet they had not been *taught* by "the grace of God . . . to say 'No' to ungodliness and worldly passions, and to live self-controlled, upright and godly lives" (Titus 2:11-12).

It is not an accident, then, that Paul does not even allude to faith, hope and love until he is two-thirds of the way through his first letter to the Corinthians. But when he does, in the last verse of the thirteenth chapter, the context is so memorable that this declaration has become one of the most well-known biblical quotations. Many pastors use 1 Corinthians 13:13 as a text for weddings and funerals, and it can be found on a variety of wall plaques in Christian bookstores.

> And now these three remain: faith, hope and love. But the greatest of these is love.

Unfortunately, many Christians do not have a clue as to what Paul really had in mind. I must admit that I did not either, until I studied these three words ("faith", "hope" and "love") in context. Then this statement became more than memorable. I discovered that Paul used this divine trilogy to evaluate the maturity level of local communities of believers. He often turned to these three words to define what it means to "become mature, attaining to the whole measure of the fullness of Christ" (Eph. 4:13; see also 3:19). Whenever he could, Paul thanked God for churches that reflected these three qualities. In fact, he boasted about these churches to others. Once I understood the broad application of these three words, it greatly marked my life and ministry as a church-planting pastor.

The Thessalonian Correspondence

Paul carried this theme through in his introductions to the Thessalonians:

> We always thank God for all of you, mentioning you in our prayers. We continually remember before our God and Father your *work produced by faith*, your *labor prompted by love*, and your *endurance inspired by hope* in our Lord Jesus Christ (1 Thess. 1:2-3).

> We ought always to thank God for you, brothers, and rightly so, because your faith is growing more and more, and the *love every one of you has for each other is increasing.* Therefore, among God's churches we boast about your perseverance and faith in all the persecutions and trials you are enduring (2 Thess. 1:3-4).

In these introductions, Paul definitely gives us some clues as to how to use these qualities to measure a church: First, he used the second person plural pronouns (you, your) to refer to the *community* of believers in Thessalonica—not just isolated individual Christians. *Together*, these Christians reflected *faith, hope* and *love*.[4]

Second, Paul succinctly defined the way each quality became visible, not only in the city of Thessalonica but throughout "Macedonia and Achaia" (1 Thess. 1:8). He referred to their: *work* produced by *faith, labor* prompted by *love, endurance* inspired by *hope*.

Third, at some point between the time Paul wrote the first and second letters to the Thessalonians, he had received a report that their *faith* was "growing more and more" and that their *love* for one another was "increasing" (2 Thess. 1:3). Consequently, he thanked God for this growth in their spiritual lives. However, he noticeably did not mention their "endurance inspired by hope"—which he thanked God for in the first letter (see 1 Thess. 1:3). There's a very important reason for this omission, and we'll explore why in chapter 7.

The Colossian Correspondence

When Paul wrote from prison in Rome to the Colossians—a church he had not yet visited—he once again referred to this divine trilogy and to commend them for their corporate maturity:[5]

> We always thank God, the Father of our Lord Jesus Christ, when we pray for you, because we have heard of your *faith* in Christ Jesus and of the *love* you have for all the saints—the *faith* and *love* that spring from the *hope* that is stored up for you in heaven (Col. 1:3-5).

Paul was overjoyed with the report he had received from Epaphras about the Colossian Christians, even though he had never met these people face-to-face (see Col. 1:7-8; 2:1). In spite of some false teachers who were attempting to confuse these believers theologically, he commended them for their *faith, hope* and *love*. You can almost feel and "see" the positive emotions reflected in Paul's countenance as he declared:

> All over the world this gospel is bearing fruit and growing, just as it has been doing among you since the day you heard it and understood God's grace in all its truth (Col. 1:6).

The Ephesian Correspondence

Ephesians is sometimes called the twin epistle to Colossians. This makes sense, not only because Paul probably wrote both letters the same year while imprisoned in Rome but also because much of what he said in both letters is similar. In some instances of the Colossian correspondence, however, Paul was quite succinct, whereas in his letter to the Ephesians he elaborated considerably on some exhortations. For example, compare what Paul wrote to various members of individual households in Colossians 3:18–4:6 with Ephesians 5:22–6:9.

There is one other unique difference in regard to Paul's reference to *faith*, *hope* and *love* in the Ephesian epistle. In his introduction to the Colossians, he *immediately* thanked God for these qualities—just as he did in his letters to the Thessalonians. However, in his letter to the Ephesians (and no doubt to the other churches in Asia), he began with an extensive reference to these believers' calling and position in Christ (Eph. 1:3-14)—and then, well into the first chapter, he thanked God first for their *faith* and *love*, followed by a prayer regarding their *hope*:

> For this reason [referring to their calling in Christ] ever since I heard about your *faith* in the Lord Jesus and your *love* for all the saints, I have not stopped giving thanks for you, remembering you in my prayers . . . . I pray also that the eyes of your heart may be enlightened in order

> that you may know the *hope* to which he has called you, the riches of his glorious inheritance in the saints (Eph. 1:15-16,18).

As we will also discover in chapter 7, there is a definite reason why Paul commended these believers for their *faith* and *love* but not their *hope* in Christ. The answer lies in understanding Paul's emphasis and concern in the rest of this epistle.

A Unique Approach

When I first began to note the introductions to Paul's letters to the Thessalonians, the Colossians and the Ephesians, I could not help but ask the question, "How did Paul begin his first letter to the Corinthians?" To be perfectly honest, I had not noticed the unique difference—and there is a difference! However, there is also one similarity. He thanked God for them (1 Cor. 1:4), a very familiar Pauline greeting (see Rom. 1:8; Eph. 1:15-16; Phil. 1:3; Col. 1:3; 1 Thess. 1:2; 2 Thess. 1:3). But clearly this is where the congruity stops. Paul's words of gratefulness moved in a much different direction, and he thanked God for the grace that had been given the Corinthians (see 1 Cor. 1:4).

This difference *is* unique, since this is the only time Paul used this greeting in his letters. When writing to the Thessalonians, the Colossians and the Ephesians, he thanked God for their faith, hope and love. However, when writing to the Corinthians, he thanked God "because of his grace" (1 Cor. 1:4) which He had bestowed on these believers when they first believed in Jesus Christ.

What does Paul mean? Was he referring to the grace, the unmerited favor, that enabled them to put their faith in Christ for salvation (Eph. 2:8-9)? Make no mistake about it. They were definitely saved by grace through faith—just as all people are. But this was not what Paul was writing about.

This leads to a second question. Was this the *grace* that had taught others "to say 'No' to ungodliness and worldly passions" (Titus 2:12)? If it were, Paul's thankfulness would have contradicted concern after concern that he spoke about in this letter. The Corinthians were definitely not living "self-controlled, upright and godly lives" (Titus 2:12).

What, then, *did* Paul have in mind? He answered this question in his very next statement. Note the following explanation in context:

> I always thank God for you because of his *grace* given you in Christ Jesus. For in him you have been enriched in every way—in all your *speaking* and in all your *knowledge*—because our testimony about Christ was confirmed in you. Therefore you do not lack any *spiritual gift* as you eagerly wait for our Lord Jesus Christ to be revealed (1 Cor. 1:4-7).

Unquestionably, Paul was referring to the "grace gifts" that the Holy Spirit had bestowed on these believers when they by faith responded to the gospel of Jesus Christ. Paul delineated

---

Though Paul thanked God for those grace gifts that confirmed their salvation, he rather quickly chided them for their carnality.

---

these gifts of the Spirit in chapters 12 through 14.[6] And, in this introductory paragraph, Paul made it very apparent that it was these *grace gifts* that had *confirmed* the gospel message and the regenerating work of the Holy Spirit in their lives.

This is the same word the author of Hebrews used to explain the purpose of "signs, wonders and various miracles, and *gifts of the Holy Spirit* distributed according to his will." They are to *confirm* the message of salvation that "was first announced by the Lord" and later proclaimed by the apostles, to "those who heard him" (Heb. 2:3-4).

This is why Paul was convinced these Corinthians were Christians, in spite of their worldly lifestyle, which could hardly be distinguished from that of their pagan neighbors. However, though he thanked God for those grace gifts that confirmed their salvation, Paul rather quickly chided them for their carnality:

> Brothers, I could not address you as spiritual but as worldly—mere infants in Christ. I gave you milk, not solid food, for you were not yet ready for it. Indeed, you are still not ready. You are still worldly. For since there is jealousy and quarreling among you, are you not worldly? Are you not acting like mere men [that is, non-Christians]? (1 Cor. 3:1-3).

The Pauline Context

Let's take a moment to reflect upon what we have observed about Paul's letters. When Paul wrote to the churches in Thessalonica, Colosse and Ephesus (and to the other churches in Asia), he began these letters by thanking God for faith, hope and love. However, when he wrote to the Corinthians, rather than thanking God for the way this divine trilogy was being reflected in their lives, he began his letter by thanking God for the grace gifts they had received when they became believers (see figure 5.1). He then proceeded to inform them of their woeful immaturity. They were still infants in Christ and were living very sinful lives—just like their unsaved neighbors. By contrast, Paul did not mention faith, hope and love until the end of chapter 13; and rather than commending them for reflecting these qualities, he reminded them that these manifestations were a true sign of maturity, not the grace gifts nor the way they were using them.

The Corinthian Context

From this *larger* context, let's look now at the *immediate* context in which Paul told the Corinthians that faith, hope and love were the true measure of maturity in a church. As we have noted, Paul began this letter by thanking God for their grace gifts. Interestingly, the first three verses of chapter 13, which we often call the great love chapter, returns to this very same theme (see figure 5.1). He acknowledged their possession and use of certain gifts but reminded them that without *love* these gifts were virtually meaningless. In essence, he was saying "Yes, you have more gifts than any church in the New Testament world ['you have been enriched in every way' (1 Cor. 1:5)] but because you lack love, your gifts are basically useless and certainly do not reflect Christ-like maturity."

As we read Paul's words in chapter 13, it is important to keep in mind the context, the concerns Paul had specifically addressed in this letter prior to this point. This church was very immature in spite of their gifts. Furthermore, Paul had just alluded to these gifts in chapter 12. Therefore, as he continued to write, he assumed the reader and the listeners would understand the continuity of his words and thoughts.

Opposite Paul's actual words in 1 Corinthians 13, in the section that follows, I have included quotes and comments that explain his succinct and summary statements in this chapter. Furthermore, in the "text" column, I have included in brackets some clear implications.

Also take note that Paul began with personal pronouns, using himself as an illustration. It seems his intent was to disarm his audience, to get them off the defensive by personally identifying with its misuse of gifts.

THEIR GIFTS WERE NOT A MEASURE OF THEIR MATURITY

1 Corinthians 13:1-3

	Paul's Text	An Explanation
13:1	If I speak in the tongues of men and of angels [like you do],	The Corinthians practiced this gift since they had *been enriched in every way—in all* [of their] *speaking* (see 1 Cor. 1:5; 14:1-25).
13:1	but have not love [like you do not],	As we will see, the Corinthians were definitely not reflecting love.
13:1	I am only a resounding gong or a clanging symbol.	The sound of their speaking gifts was as noise without true meaning because of their lack of love.
13:2	If I have the gift of prophecy and can fathom all mysteries and all knowledge [like you do],	The Corinthians practiced these gifts as well (see 1 Cor. 12:1-30).
13:2	and if I have a faith that can move mountains, but have not love [like you do not],	Even if they had this kind of faith-gift, they still lacked the most important quality of maturity: the love of Christ.
13:2	I am nothing.	The way they were using these gifts (prophesying, knowledge, faith) was a meaningless exercise in God's sight.

13:3	If I give all I possess to the poor and surrender my body to the flames, but have not love [like you do not] I gain nothing.	The Corinthians could have given away all their material possessions and even died as martyrs, but since they still lacked love, this kind of sacrifice would accomplish nothing in God's sight.

Become a Corinthian

Imagine, if you can, that you were one of the Corinthians listening to this letter being read. You thought that the giftedness in your church was the true measure of spirituality. However, Paul is telling you that what you and your fellow Corinthians value the most means very little in God's sight. The gifts you are so proud of are simply a reflection of God's grace—not a mature response to His grace.

The most painful reality, however, would be to hear Paul declare that you and your church lacked love. A natural reaction would be to rationalize or to question Paul's conclusion, especially since some of you do not even avow to follow the apostle Paul anymore. Some of you claim Apollos as your mentor. Others of you follow Cephas, or Peter as your spiritual leader. Others simply boast that they follow Christ (see 1 Cor. 1:12). Since you were already carnal, you would probably at this point become even more carnal—and very angry.

Paul, in his Spirit-directed wisdom, anticipated the various reactions from the Corinthians. This is why he proceeded to use a literary technique that must have left them rather speechless and unable to continue to rationalize. Within the space of just four verses, he reviewed almost sequentially (chapter by chapter) all of the major marks of immaturity that he had addressed in the first 12 chapters of this letter—issues and problems in their lives that demonstrated unequivocally why they were not demonstrating love. It is as if Paul stated: "I know some of you are sad and even angry because I told you that love is missing from your lives. So let me tell you why you have no love. I have told you already in this letter, but let me review for you what I've written."

THEIR LOVE WAS VIRTUALLY NONEXISTENT

1 CORINTHIANS 13:4-6

	Paul's Text	An Explanation
13:4	Love is patient, love is kind. It does not envy,	In chapter 3, Paul told them they were impatient, unkind and envious. Specifically he wrote: "You are still worldly. For since there is jealousy and quarreling among you, are you not worldly?" (1 Cor. 3:3).
13:4	[love] does not boast, it is not proud.	In chapters 3 and 4, Paul told them they were demonstrating the opposite of love. Specifically he wrote: "So then, no more boasting about men!" (1 Cor. 3:21) and "Some of you have become arrogant, as if I were not coming to you" (1 Cor. 4:18).
13:5	[Love] is not rude, it is not self-seeking,	In chapter 11, Paul described the ultimate in rudeness and self-seeking: "When you come together, it is not the Lord's Supper you eat, for as you eat, each of you goes ahead without waiting for anybody else. One remains hungry, another gets drunk" (1 Cor. 11:20-21).

13:5	[love] is not easily angered, it keeps no record of wrongs.	In chapter 6, Paul described their anger against one another: "If any of you has a dispute with another, dare he take it before the ungodly for judgment instead of before the saints? . . . But instead, one brother goes to law against another–and this in front of unbelievers!" (1 Cor. 6:1,6).
13:6	Love does not delight in evil but rejoices with the truth.	In chapter 5 and 6, Paul referred to their immoral behavior: "It is actually reported that there is sexual immorality among you. . . . Do you not know that your bodies are members of Christ himself? Shall I then take the members of Christ and unite them with a prostitute? Never! . . . You were bought at a price. Therefore honor God with your body (1 Cor. 5:1; 6:15,20).
13:7	[Love] always protects,	In chapter 8, Paul chided them for not caring about their weaker brothers when they purchased meat offered to idols: "Be careful, however, that the exercise of your freedom does not become a stumbling block to the weak" (1 Cor. 8:9).
13:7	[love] always trusts,	In chapter 9, Paul had to defend his apostleship. They no longer trusted the one who led them to Christ: "Are you not the result of my work in the Lord? Even though I may not be an apostle to others, surely I am to you! For you are the seal of my apostleship in the Lord" (1 Cor. 9:1-2).

13:7 [love] always hopes.	In chapter 15, Paul addressed the fact that some no longer believed in the resurrection of Christ—the basis of a Christian's hope: "And if Christ has not been raised, your faith is futile; you are still in your sins. Then those also who have fallen asleep in Christ are lost. If only for this life we have hope in Christ, we are to be pitied more than all men" (1 Cor. 15:17-19).

Within the space of four verses, Paul shows that the Corinthians had little, if any, love. If they were listening at all, they could not deny this indictment. They were:

- Impatient
- Unkind
- Envious
- Boastful
- Vengeful
- Rejecting truth
- Untrusting
- Proud
- Rude
- Self-seeking
- Easily angered
- Encouraging immorality
- Stumbling blocks to other Christians
- Denying the resurrection

Paul not only summarized their lack of love, but he also noted their self-centered focus (their own giftedness) and reminded them that these gifts were merely temporal and only a means to develop spiritual maturity. These gifts were to prepare them for that glorious day when they would be transformed into the image of Christ. The Corinthians had allowed their supernatural grace gifts to become ends in themselves and to become expressions of arrogance, leading to division and disunity. Paul explained why they should pursue faith, hope and love.

THEIR FOCUS WAS MISDIRECTED

1 CORINTHIANS 13:8-13

	Paul's Text	An Explanation
13:7-8	[Love] always perseveres. Love never fails. But where there are prophecies, they will cease;	Their prophecy gifts were temporal, whereas love is eternal.
13:8	where there are tongues, they will be stilled;	Their tongue gifts were temporal, whereas love is eternal.
13:8	where there is knowledge, it will pass away.	Their knowledge gifts were temporal, whereas love is eternal.
13:9-10	For we know in part and we prophesy in part but, when perfection comes, the imperfect disappears.	Paul seemed to be using the word "perfection" in this context to refer to their total transformation into the image of Christ at the Second Coming. At that moment, the temporal or the "imperfect" will cease to exist. Then "we will be changed" (1 Cor. 15:52). We will see Christ "face-to-face" (1 Cor. 13:12).[7]
13:11	When I was a child, I talked like a child, I thought like a child,	Paul used his personal life as an illustration to tell them that he once was like them—acting like

	Paul's Text	An Explanation
	I reasoned like a child. When I became a man, I put childish ways behind me.	child. But when he began to measure up to the fullness of Christ, he no longer focused on his gifts, but on developing faith, hope and love, but especially love.
13:12	Now we see but a poor reflection as in a mirror; then we shall see face-to-face.	Their corporate lifestyle was a very poor reflection of Christ as they looked into the mirror of God's truth. What came back from the mirror was impatience, unkindness, jealousy, bragging, arrogance, etc. (see figure 5.2). There was little "fruit of the Spirit"—only their carnal attitudes and actions. However, some day they would be transformed into Christ's likeness. There will be no mirror, for they will see Jesus Christ face-to-face and they will be like Him. This is the "perfection" they would see and some day experience (see 1 Cor. 13:9 and figure 5.3).
13:12	Now I know in part; then I shall know fully, even as I am fully known.	At that moment their knowledge of God was limited, but when they were transformed into His image, they would have full knowledge.
13:13	And now these three remain: faith, hope and love. But the greatest of these is love.	They did not need to continue as things were. From this point forward, they could focus on what is most important: faith, hope and love—but especially love.

Guiding Principles

Principle 1. When measuring a church, we must not evaluate spirituality by a manifestation of spiritual gifts.

The Corinthians were certainly one of the most gifted churches in the New Testament era. Yet, they were the most immature and worldly. The fact that they were using these gifts extensively was not evidence of their spiritual maturity.

This leads to a very important biblical observation that speaks directly to some Christians' theological confusion. The Corinthian church demonstrates conclusively that *spiritual gifts* and *spiritual maturity* are not automatically synonymous. It is possible to be extremely gifted, yet carnal and worldly. It is difficult to understand how true believers could be speaking in tongues, prophesying, uttering words of knowledge and delivering words of wisdom, yet still be practicing immoral behavior, getting drunk at the communion meal and suing one another in pagan courts. Yet this was undeniably true among the Corinthians, even five to six years after they had become believers.

Thankfully, at some point, they began to respond to the truth, which is obvious in 2 Corinthians. Paul does not yet commend them for faith, hope and love, but he did state the following:

> Even if I caused you sorrow by my letter, I do not regret it. Though I did regret it–I see that my letter hurt you, but only for a little while–yet now I am happy, not because you were made sorry, but because your sorrow led you to repentance. For you became sorrowful as God intended and so were not harmed in any way by us (2 Cor. 7:8-9).[8]

In recent years, there has been a renewed emphasis on the gifts of the Spirit. Furthermore, these gifts are often classified as a sign of spirituality. Some go as far as to say that if certain gifts are not obvious, a church is not a Spirit-filled church. The direct implication is that if the church is not Spirit filled, it is definitely deficient in spirituality.

Sadly, this emphasis sometimes leads to the same attitudes and behaviors that existed in the Corinthian church: confusion, pride, arrogance and judgmental attitudes. Unfortunately, it also sometimes leads to the worst kind of rationalization: justifying sinful behavior. It has been argued, "How could I have this particular gift of the Spirit if God were not pleased with my homosexual relationship?" Although this may seem to be an extreme example, it has been heard again and again by pastors everywhere. People also attempt to justify premarital sex, adultery and non-biblical divorce. This should not surprise us, since it happened in the Corinthian church. In fact, it happened so often that Paul stated that if it were not for their gifts, he would not have known they were true Christians.

On the other hand, this kind of sinful behavior is not just present in churches that confuse spiritual gifts and true spirituality. The same shortcomings are present in other churches that proclaim the true gospel of God's grace but downplay the gifts of the Spirit or deny that they exist. People have accepted Jesus Christ by faith, and yet they are not living Christlike lives. The same sins permeate the congregation. They claim to be born again by the Spirit, yet they are not living "by the Spirit" (see Gal. 5:16,25). They, too, are immature and carnal. They are still conformed to the pattern of this world. They have not yet offered their bodies as living sacrifices, holy and pleasing to God. They are not living in the "good, pleasing and perfect will" of God (Rom. 12:2).

Focusing on Maturity

Let me share a personal experience: When I first began to explore in-depth what the New Testament has to say about the church, I discovered in a new way the concept of spiritual gifts. Consequently, I began to emphasize these gifts, challenging Christians to discover their gifts and to use them.

Frankly, I was surprised by the response. I saw Christians who became confused. Some claimed that their natural abilities were "gifts." Some believed they had gifts when they obviously didn't. Others rationalized and put aside clear biblical responsibilities as a Christian because they had certain gifts and not others.

When we stress what God stresses, we eliminate confusion and create unity in the Body of Jesus Christ.

Amidst these various responses to my teaching on gifts, I looked at the New Testament again and discovered that the Bible does not emphasize looking for gifts; rather, it underscores the importance of becoming mature in Christ. This insight changed my focus, and not surprisingly, it changed the way Christians began to function in my church. The confusion subsided and I saw more people than ever begin to do God's work in God's way. This is to be expected. When we stress what God stresses, we eliminate confusion and create unity in the Body of Jesus Christ.

The Degree of Faith, Hope and Love

Principle 2. When measuring a church, we must look for the degree to which believers are manifesting faith, hope and love—but especially love.

A comparison of Paul's letter to the Corinthians with his letters to the Thessalonians, the Colossians and the Ephesians demonstrates clearly that we should measure the maturity level of a local church by the degree of faith, hope and love that is expressed and reflected in that church. In essence, this is the kind of corporate lifestyle that demonstrates the extent to which a body of Christians is "attaining to the whole measure of the fullness of Christ." In other words, the degree of faith, hope and love indicates the extent to which believers are living "by the Spirit," rather than manifesting the "acts of the sinful nature" (see Gal. 5:16-26).

It is God's will, of course, that each believer in a corporate body reflects these qualities. However, it is possible for a church to demonstrate faith, hope and love, even though in any given church there will be immature believers (new Christians), carnal Christians (those who live after the flesh rather than the Spirit) and even "natural" or unsaved people (particularly those who are seeking God). In fact, any church that is really impacting the world will include these three groups of people. But at the same time, if the church as a whole is growing spiritually, the *committed core* of that church will be a reflection of Jesus Christ and His lifestyle. Unfortunately, the Corinthians did not have a committed core. If they had, Paul certainly would have commended them.

Furthermore, that church will be the best place for those who lack faith, hope and love to grow and mature in these areas of their lives to mingle with and observe the committed core who are walking in the light and measuring up to the fullness of Christ. In fact, it is in this context that God has planned that true discipleship take place—within a functioning body that is "joined and held together by every supporting ligament." It is then that the "whole body . . . grows and builds itself up in love, as each part does its work" (Eph. 4:16).

The apostle Peter zeroed in on the same qualities when he wrote to the churches "scattered throughout Pontus, Galatia, Cappadocia, Asia and Bithynia" (1 Pet.1:1). In the following paragraph, you will see that he not only emphasized the three qualities of maturity–faith, hope and love–but he also made it clear that "the greatest of these is love":

> Through him [Christ] you believe in God, who raised him from the dead and glorified him, and so *your faith* and *hope* are in God. Now that you have purified yourselves by obeying the truth so that you have *sincere love* for your brothers, *love one another* deeply, from the heart (1 Pet. 1:21-22).

There are a lot of ways churches are measured today. We have noted that an emphasis on gifts is not a true measurement of spirituality. But there are other criteria that are promoted. The most prominent are good Bible teaching, evangelistic preaching, numerical growth, building projects, well-orchestrated services, contemporary music, need-oriented music, a seeker-sensitive environment, a potpourri of activities, a mission outreach, organizational efficiency, management styles and countless others. All of these things are noteworthy, and most are even important, but these things are not what Paul and other New Testament writers thanked God for in their letters to New Testament churches. Rather, they were thankful for the degree of faith, hope and love that existed in those churches.

If Paul sat down and addressed a letter to your church, how would he begin the letter? What would he thank God for? I often ask myself these questions about the church that I pastor.

Thinking and Growing Together

1. From your experience, what happens in a church when spiritual gifts are emphasized? Has this led to some of the same problems we have seen in the Corinthian church? If it has not, why not?
2. From your experience, what happens in a church that does not emphasize gifts? Has this led to true spirituality? If not, why not?
3. From your experience, have you ever been in a church that emphasizes faith, hope and love as the true measure of maturity? Did this emphasis lead to Christlike attitudes and behavior? If not, why not?

Figure 5.1 Biblical Measurements of Maturity

Figure 5.2

Figure 5.3

Notes

1. Gordon D. Fee, *The New International Commentary on the New Testament: The First Epistle to the Corinthians* (Grand Rapids, MI: Wm. B. Eerdmans Publishing Company, 1987), p. 651.
2. C. K. Barrett, *The First Epistle to the Corinthians* (Peabody, MA: Hendrickson Publishers, 1968), p. 310.
3. W. Harold Mare, *Expositor's Bible Commentary,* ed. Frank E. Gaebelein, vol. 10 (Grand Rapids, MI: Zondervan Publishing House, 1976), p. 205.
4. When we read the Bible in English, it is difficult to discern between singular and plural pronouns, since we use the same words ("you", "your") to refer both to individuals and to groups. In the Greek language this distinction is clear. This is true of the original New Testament text. In general, most "you" and "your" pronouns are plural unless statements are directed toward individuals. This is significant, since biblical writers often refer to community manifestations of maturity rather than just personal reflections of it.
5. Although Paul and other New Testament writers used plural pronouns most frequently to describe the manifestation of faith, hope and love, this does not mean these qualities cannot be attributed to an individual. This is clear in Paul's letter to Philemon, who also lived in Colosse. In this letter, Paul used singular pronouns: "I always thank my God as I remember you in my prayers, because I hear about your faith in the Lord Jesus and your love for all the saints" (Philem. 4-5).
6. See chapter 4 for additional biblical references that associate spiritual gifts with God's special grace.
7. It is my personal opinion that this passage of Scripture cannot be used exegetically to teach that gifts have now ceased. By "temporal," I'm referring to life as we know it on Earth. Since God is love, this quality will endure forever. We must remember that when Paul wrote 1 Corinthians, he no doubt believed Jesus Christ was going to return in his lifetime–and from his perspective, very soon (see 1 Cor. 15:51-52). He did not anticipate that the Corinthians' gifts would disappear before this great moment. The fact that Paul was limited in his knowledge of Christ's return in no way affected the divine inspiration of Scripture. We see the same phenomena in the Old Testament when the prophets spoke of the coming of Christ but confused the two comings–the first, when He born as a babe in Bethlehem and the second, when He comes as King of kings and Lord of lords. Yet, in spite of this limited knowledge, Paul spoke the infallible Word of the Lord.
8. Most Bible interpreters agree that the letter Paul referred to in 2 Corinthians is not 1 Corinthians. Rather, it is a lost letter Paul wrote after a painful visit. When Paul heard how much sorrow the letter caused, which must have been far more pointed than 1 Corinthians, he referenced that sorrow in 2 Corinthians 7:8-9.

CHAPTER 6

FAITH THAT WORKS

New Testament writers used the word "faith" (*pistis*) and its synonym "believe" (*pisteuo*) nearly 500 times—approximately 250 times each. Such repetition demonstrates how basic and important this concept is in Scripture.

It is not accidental, then, that when *faith*, *hope* and *love* are combined as criteria for measuring a church, the concept of *faith* usually appears first. Paul verified the importance of this sequence in his first letter to the Corinthians, "Now these three remain: *faith*, [followed by] *hope* and *love*" (1 Cor. 13:13).

FOUR PERSPECTIVES

Faith is foundational in Christian living. Without it, the Bible declares that it "is impossible to please God" (Heb. 11:6). To better understand faith, let's look at four invaluable insights into this cornerstone of our relationship with God.

Saving Faith

Faith that regenerates and serves as a means of salvation takes us once again to Paul's great declaration in his letter to the Ephesians:

> For it is by grace you have been saved, *through faith*—and this not from yourselves, it is the gift of God—not by works, so that no one can boast (Eph. 2:8-9).

Paul and other authors of Scripture supported and confirmed this great truth with dozens of other statements. In fact, we have already seen in chapter 4 that Paul's major purpose when he wrote the Galatian letter was to explain and clarify that salvation is a matter of faith, not works. Three times in this letter alone Paul asserted that we are "justified by *faith*" (Gal. 3:24, see also 2:16; 3:8).

In his Gospel, John used one form or another of the word "believe" (*pisteuo*) 98 times as a synonym for faith. In most cases he demonstrated that we are "saved by grace through faith." A classic example is found in John 3:16: "For God so loved the world that he gave his one and only Son, that whoever *believes* in him shall not perish but have eternal life." This, of course, was the purpose of John's Gospel—that we might "*believe* that Jesus is the Christ, the Son of God, and that by *believing* you [we] may have life in his name" (John 20:31).

The Faith

New Testament writers also used the word "faith" to refer to a system of beliefs (a body of truth). For example, someone might ask you: "What is *your faith*?" In reality, that person is asking what your particular church believes. He or she is inquiring about your tradition, your denomination or your religious affiliation and might even ask you about your church's doctrinal statement.

There is a biblical precedent for these questions. New Testament writers used the phrase "*the faith*" to refer to what true Christians believe.

A large number of priests became obedient to *the faith* (Acts 6:7).

In the early days of Christianity, many Jewish priests zealously opposed and rejected the teachings of the apostles, specifically the assertion that Jesus Christ was indeed the true Messiah, the Promised One who was crucified, buried, resurrected and ascended to the right hand of the Father. However, not all of the religious leaders resisted this message. Rather, many became "obedient to *the faith*," which means they embraced the *doctrines* of Christianity.

The man who formerly persecuted us is now preaching the faith he once tried to destroy (Gal. 1:23).

Paul wrote this about his own conversion. Prior to his encounter with Jesus Christ on the road to Damascus, he did all that he could to stop Christians from communicating the gospel of Christ. But once Paul had been converted, he became one of the most ardent propagators of the Christian faith! He did not discard his Jewish faith, but he understood that the demands of the Old Testament law were fulfilled in Jesus Christ when He died on the cross for the sins of the world (see Gal. 3:10-14). He explained this to the Galatians when he wrote, "Christ redeemed us from the curse of the law by becoming a curse for us" (Gal. 3:13).

[God will build up the Body of Christ] until we all reach unity in the faith and in the knowledge of the Son of God and become mature, attaining to the whole measure of fullness of the Christ (Eph. 4:13).

Here Paul was referring primarily to basic doctrinal unity. Creating unity is one of our important tasks as pastors and teachers. There are, of course, peripheral issues where honest Christians disagree, but there are foundational beliefs that cannot be compromised. For example, we cannot teach that a person is saved by his or her works. The Bible clearly declares that salvation comes by faith alone.

Closely aligned with this foundational doctrine is the teaching on the Trinity. God is three Persons: Father, Son and Holy Spirit, and yet one God. Most religious groups that depart from this classical Christian theology have developed a false view of the Trinity. When this happens, it also affects that group's doctrine of salvation. When people have a false view of this "eternal community" (Father, Son and Holy Spirit), they usually also misunderstand why Jesus came and what He really meant when He said, "I am the way and the truth and the life. No one comes to the Father except through me" (John 14:6).

Doctrine on the second coming of Christ is also essential and foundational in Christianity. Believers certainly vary in their opinions as to *when* Jesus Christ will come, but we must never waver on the great truth that *He is coming*. In fact, as we will note in the next chapter, this important truth is indispensable if Christians are to have a true sense of *hope*.

Without unity in the faith regarding these and other essential doctrines (see Eph. 4:13), Christians are like "infants, tossed back and forth by the waves, and blown here and there by *every wind of teaching*" (Eph. 4:14). This is why in the church I pastor we have a basic interactive course called Discovery that is designed to ground Christians in the foundational truths of Scripture, beginning with how to be truly saved!

The Gift of Faith

When Paul wrote to the Corinthians, he referred to the gift of "*faith*" (1 Cor. 12:9). Interestingly, this is the only specific reference to this gift, and as was noted in chapter 5, this manifestation was not necessarily associated with Christian maturity. The Corinthians had many gifts, yet they were the most carnal and immature church in the New Testament world.

At the same time, there were mature Christian men such as Stephen who may have had the gift of faith. Stephen was chosen to help meet the needs of the Grecian widows in Jerusalem and is identified as "a man full of faith and of the Holy Spirit" (Acts 6:5). When the apostles chose Barnabas to go to Antioch to help establish the church there, he was also described as a man of faith: "He was a good man, *full of the Holy Spirit and faith*" (Acts 11:24). If these men indeed had the gift of faith, they were definitely using this gift to build up the Body of Jesus Christ, not themselves.

Living Faith

When Paul and other New Testament writers refer to faith as it is used in the divine trilogy, they primarily refer to living faith. It is this kind of faith that reflects a very important dimension of maturity for individuals and, more importantly, for a *community* of believers. Most references to this kind of faith have a corporate dimension. Jesus referred to this expression of community experience when He said, "For where two or three come together in my name, there am I with them" (Matt. 18:20). Jesus, of course, is always with us as individual believers, but when *in faith*, we pray together, His presence is unleashed in dynamic ways.

Living faith is to be an ongoing spiritual experience. When it exists and grows, it definitely reflects maturity in a local body of believers. Of course, this level of faith is impossible without saving faith. Once we are saved by grace through faith, living faith builds upon this foundation of saving faith.

This living faith is also intricately related to *what we believe*, which is identified in the Scriptures as "the faith." We see this interrelatedness when Paul encouraged the Ephesians to "take up the *shield of faith*" (Eph. 6:16), a metaphor that no doubt includes all dimensions of faith. However, Paul was certainly focusing specifically on living faith, which is a way for a body of believers to defeat Satan in their walk with Christ.[1]

The Thessalonian Correspondence

When Paul wrote his first letter to the Thessalonians, he thanked God for their "work produced by faith" (1 Thess. 1:3). A work produced by faith means a living faith. Although succinct, this reference is a foundational definition: Living faith reflects works. It is an extension of saving faith. This is what Paul had in mind in that great declaration in Ephesians where he said that we are saved "by grace . . . through faith." We cannot earn salvation "by works" (Eph. 2:9)! However, Paul then takes us beyond our salvation experience and reminds us that "we are God's *workmanship*, created in Christ Jesus to *do good works*" (Eph. 2:10). And these "good works" are a reflection of spiritual growth.

Paul was simply affirming what James had written earlier: "Faith by itself, if it is not accompanied by action, is dead" (James 2:17). James also wrote, "As the body without the spirit is dead, so faith without deeds is dead" (2:26). In other words, true saving faith will eventually result in good works, a reflection of living faith. This is God's eternal plan. A. Skevington Wood put it well: "The road is already built."[2] As believers, we are to walk that road.

The Christian Walk

Throughout the Ephesian letter, Paul used a metaphorical word that helps us understand more fully what he had in mind when he thanked God for "the work of faith" in the church in Thessalonica. The Greek word is *peripateo*, which literally means "to tread about," or "to walk." Paul used this word to describe how Christians are to live out their salvation experience. In fact, the *New International Version* translates this as "to do" after we are saved. In context, Paul wrote, "We are God's *workmanship*, created in Christ Jesus *to do* [*peripateo*] good works" (Eph. 2:10). Not only has God saved us, but He has also made provision to enable us to walk along a certain path. When we do, particularly as a community of faith, others will see our work produced by faith.

Paul continued to use this basic word "*peripateo*" to exhort New Testament believers *to do* these good works. The translators of the *New King James Version* capture the beauty of the metaphor in the last chapters of Ephesians:

> I, therefore, the prisoner of the Lord, beseech you *to have a walk worthy of the calling* with which you were called (4:1, *NKJV*).

> This I say, therefore, and testify in the Lord, that you should *no longer walk* as the rest of the Gentiles *walk*, in the futility of their mind (4:17, *NKJV*).

> Therefore be followers of God as dear children. And *walk in love*, as Christ also has loved us and given Himself up for us (5:1-2, *NKJV*).

> For you were once darkness, but now you are light in the Lord. *Walk as children of light* (for the fruit of the Spirit is in all goodness, righteousness, and truth) (5:8-9, *NKJV*).

> See then that you *walk circumspectly*, not as fools but as wise, redeeming the time, because the days are evil (5:15-16, *NKJV*).

When Christians "walk worthy," as Paul described it, they are demonstrating "work produced by faith" (1 Thess. 1:3) This is in essence why Paul was commending the Thessalonians. He had heard about the way they had left the "broad . . . road that leads

When Christians "walk worthy," as Paul described it, they are demonstrating "work produced by faith."

to destruction" and were traveling down the "narrow . . . road that leads to life" (Matt. 7:13-14). They were walking the path Jesus described as "the way and the truth and the life" (John 14:6). He, of course, was—and still is—that path.

The Thessalonians, then, are a positive example of believers who were reflecting a living faith through their walk with Christ. In fact, it was a growing work of faith. This is why
mended them once again in his second letter. Their faith was "growing more and more" (2 Thess. 1:3). In other words, their

"work produced by faith" was becoming even more obvious. Unlike the Corinthians, they were moving beyond infancy into adulthood, no longer talking like children, thinking like children and reasoning like children. They were starting to put their childish ways behind them (see 1 Cor. 13:11).

A More Specific Reflection of Faith

Paul's reflection on the "work produced by faith" among the Thessalonians had an even more specific focus. When he had secretly left the city of Thessalonica because of intense persecution (see Acts 17:5-10), he was deeply concerned about the effect this continued persecution would have on these new believers. Would they continue to be strong in their faith? Would Satan sidetrack them and hinder the work Paul and his fellow missionaries had begun?

When Paul arrived at Athens, his anxiety level was so intense that he and Silas sent Timothy back to Thessalonica. He had one major purpose: "to strengthen and encourage" them in their "faith" (1 Thess. 3:2). Later, when Timothy had returned with a good report, Paul penned these words reflecting upon his own concerns and subsequent action:

> But Timothy has just now come to us from you and has brought good news about *your faith*. . . . Therefore, brothers, in all our distress and persecution we were encouraged about you because of *your faith* (1 Thess. 3:6-7).

What were some of the specific visible and measurable aspects of their "work produced by faith" that Paul mentioned in this letter? First, those who had been converted out of paganism had not returned to their idolatrous and immoral lifestyles (see 1 Thess. 1:8-10). In fact, by the time Paul wrote his first letter, their faith in God had become known all over Macedonia and was even being talked about in the neighboring country of Achaia (see 1 Thess. 1:5-7). With this reference to their faith, Paul was not only referring to their salvation experience (saving faith) but also to what they believed (*the* faith) and to the way they were walking by faith (living faith).

Second, these believers reflected their "work produced by faith" by continuing to serve Jesus Christ in spite of persecution. They had not turned their backs on God and denied that they knew and loved Him. This is certainly inherent in the encouraging report Timothy shared with Paul and Silas. Paul responded with these glowing words:

> For now we really live, since you are standing firm in the Lord (1 Thess. 3:8).

Third, the Thessalonians, along with other churches, reflected their living faith with their generous and sacrificial spirit in sharing their material possessions. Though Paul was probably not referring particularly to this "work produced by faith" in his initial letters to the Thessalonians, he notes their generosity in his second letter to the Corinthians, which was written five or six years after his Thessalonian correspondence. At some point in time, Paul returned to this church and the other churches in Macedonia (no doubt the Thessalonians, the Philippians and the Bereans) and challenged them to help their fellow believers who were suffering throughout Judea. In spite of their own physical needs, these believers responded to this challenge. When Paul wrote to the Corinthians, he used the "work produced by *faith*" in these Macedonian churches as a model of generosity. Few churches in the Western world today can even identify with the sacrificial giving that Paul connotes in his second letter to the Corinthians:

> And now, brothers, we want you to know about the grace that God has given the Macedonian churches. Out of the most severe trial, their overflowing joy and their extreme poverty welled up in rich generosity. For I testify that they gave as much as they were able, and even beyond their ability. Entirely on their own, they urgently pleaded with us for the privilege of sharing in this service to the saints (8:1-4).

If Paul had written a third letter to the Thessalonian believers, he would certainly have again commended them for the way their faith continued to grow, especially in view of this kind of generosity.

The Hebrew Correspondence

Theologians are not sure who wrote the book of Hebrews. Personally, I favor the idea that it was Apollos, a Jewish believer who, along with Priscilla and Aquila, ministered with Paul (see Acts 18:24-28).

Consequently, as we delve into Hebrews, I will take the liberty of using Apollos's name as the author. While scholars debate who wrote this document, I must admit that the more I use his name in association with the content in Hebrews, the more feasible it seems that he may have actually penned it. The truths this book unfolds seem to fit his personal intellectual and spiritual journey.

The author of Hebrews, of course, speaks to a great extent about the way Jesus Christ has fulfilled the law and the sacrificial system in the Old Testament. This certainly fits Apollos's background as a dedicated Jew. Furthermore, we are told that the Greek text is exquisite, the product of a very intelligent man. This would certainly correlate with the fact that Apollos grew up in

Alexandria, a great center of Greek learning. Furthermore, Apollos's close association with Paul may explain why some sections of this letter mirror the apostle's expressions. Yet, overall the content is unique. (I have put Apollos's name in quotation marks to acknowledge that the authorship is actually undetermined.)

Infants in Christ

In some respects, the believers to whom "Apollos" was writing were like the Corinthians. They were "slow to learn," and they needed "milk, not solid food!" (Heb. 5:11-12; see 1 Cor. 3:1-4). They were not yet able to handle the deep truths of God's Word, particularly regarding godly living. Mixing metaphors with pointed applications, "Apollos" drove home his point:

> Anyone who lives on *milk*, being still an *infant*, is not acquainted with the teaching about righteousness. But solid food is for the *mature*, who by constant use have trained themselves to distinguish good from evil (see Heb. 5:13-14).

The Divine Trilogy

The author's purpose, however, was not to be critical; rather it was to challenge these believing communities to "leave the elementary teachings about Christ and go on to maturity" (Heb. 6:1). In other words, they were to grow up spiritually. After carefully explaining that Christ is the great high priest and the one, final and perfect sacrifice for sins, he went on to spell out the true criteria for measuring maturity in a body of believers. What he stated, in view of what we have already noted in Paul's letters, should not surprise us:

> Let us draw near to God with a sincere heart in full assurance of *faith*. . . . Let us hold unswervingly to the

hope we profess, for he who promised is faithful. And let us consider how we may spur one another on toward *love* and good deeds (Heb. 10:22-24).

Once again we see the unity of Scripture. The author of Hebrews is in perfect alignment with Paul and Peter regarding the basic criteria for measuring a church: the degree of faith, hope and love that is expressed in that body of believers.

A Foundational Concern

"Apollos," however, had a foundational concern. These believers needed to give attention to "work produced by faith." Evidently they were wavering because of increased persecution. Consequently, "Apollos" reminded them of the "earlier days" when they first became believers–when they had accepted Jesus Christ as the promised Messiah (see Heb. 10:32). Although they had obviously regressed spiritually, there was a time when they had stood strong in their faith, in spite of severe suffering. When they had been lined up with others who were being insulted and persecuted, they had not retreated. They had ministered to fellow Christians who had been incarcerated, and when their own property had been confiscated, they were able to rejoice (see Heb. 10:32-34).

It is then revealed *why* these believers had been able to face these difficult trials with glad hearts. Their *faith* had been strong and vibrant. They *knew* in their hearts they "had better and lasting possessions" (Heb. 10:34).

But things changed, and at this point, "Apollos" encouraged these wavering believers to return to the same living faith they had in those early days and to not throw away their confidence. They were exhorted to persevere in doing the will of God, remembering that the Lord would not renege on His promises–the rewards He will someday give those who faithfully serve Him, especially in difficult circumstances.

Illustrations of Faith

To encourage these believers, "Apollos" dips back into Old Testament history and illustrates his message with powerful "examples of faith." He mentioned all of the patriarchs, and he even included Rahab the prostitute because of her faith in the God of Abraham, Isaac and Jacob (see Heb. 11:4-31).

"Apollos" concluded this list of examples by reminding New Testament believers that all of these Old Testament saints kept trusting God even though they never saw many of God's promises materialize in their lifetime. They looked to the future, knowing that the Lord is always faithful.

"Apollos" called these examples of faith "a great cloud of witnesses" (Heb. 12:1) and he challenged these Hebrew believers to such unwavering trust in God. He then outlined two important lessons in faith.

Lesson One: Be Unencumbered

First, we must lay aside everything that keeps us from reaching the goal of becoming mature in Christ. Consequently, "Apollos" wrote, "Let us throw off everything that hinders and the sin that so easily entangles" (Heb. 12:1).

Clearly, the author was referring to the sins that can exist in our lives as believers. And to make his point more apparent, he spelled out exactly what these sins are!

Bitterness

Bitterness destroys *faith* rather than builds it. When Christians get their eyes on each other's faults rather than on the perfection of Jesus Christ, there is only one result: distrust and disillusionment. Consequently, Apollos wrote:

> See to it that . . . *no bitter root grows up* to cause trouble and defile many (Heb. 12:15).

Immorality

In the New Testament world, immorality was the norm. But wherever the Christian message was proclaimed, a new value system was taught. This was a value system that emaphasized sexual purity. The gift of sex was for marriage. Within this God-ordained relationship, sex was good, beautiful and proper. In fact, failure to engage in a sexual relationship within marriage was a sin, both against God and the marital partner (see 1 Cor. 7:1-7). But outside of marriage, a sexual relationship was out of the will of God and a complete distortion of what God had in mind for two people who have entered into a lifetime commitment. To underscore this point, "Apollos" exhorted:

> See that no one is sexually immoral. . . . Marriage should be honored by all, and the marriage bed kept pure, for God will judge the adulterer and all the sexually immoral (Heb. 12:16; 13:4).

Immorality, like bitterness, destroys faith rather than builds it. Because of its guilt-producing effects, it militates against drawing "near to God with a *sincere heart* in *full assurance of faith*, having our hearts sprinkled to cleanse us from a *guilty conscience*" (Heb. 10:22).

Materialism

The Bible does not teach that as believers we are to be free from money; rather, we are to be free from "the love of money" (Heb. 13:5), which is materialism. The Bible does not even teach that it is wrong to accumulate money, unless the motive is to substitute material wealth for a dependence on God. "Apollos" was concerned about the sin of materialism in the churches he was addressing. Consequently, he wrote:

> Keep your lives free from the *love of money* and be content with what you have, because God has said, "Never will I leave you; never will I forsake you" (Heb. 13:5).

The book of Hebrews reinforces what Jesus Christ taught: "You cannot serve both God and money" (Matt. 6:24). Rather, as believers we are to "seek first his kingdom and his righteousness, and all these things will be given to you [us] as well" (Matt. 6:33).

Legalism

In the midst of their persecution, the Hebrew Christians lapsed into legalism, perhaps because of their insecurity. They reverted to old patterns and practices, trying to find the strength to face

---

The book of Hebrews reinforces what Jesus Christ taught: "You cannot serve both God and money."

---

their trials—in one case, partaking of ceremonial foods. This development, of course, also worked against the biblical concept of *faith*. Consequently, "Apollos" wrote:

> It is good for our hearts to be *strengthened by grace*, not *by ceremonial foods*, which are of no value to those who eat them (Heb. 13:9; see also Gal. 5:5-6).

Lesson Two: Eyes on the Goal

Using an athletic metaphor to make his point, "Apollos" reminded believers that a runner always looks straight ahead. If the crowd's cheers or jeers distract a racer, he might fall behind. Applying this to the Church, the author of Hebrews exhorted:

> Let us fix our eyes on Jesus, *the author and perfecter* of our faith (Heb. 12:2).

As Christians, if we are going to demonstrate a strong and dynamic "work produced by *faith*" (1 Thess. 1:3) that is "growing more and more" (2 Thess. 1:3), we must keep our eyes on our goal, which is to become like Jesus Christ. He is our great example of humility and unselfishness (see Phil. 2:3-8). He ran this race and He won it. He went before us. He can identify with every problem or temptation we face, including fear, weariness and pride. He became like us "in order that he might become a merciful and faithful high priest. . . . Because he himself suffered when he was tempted, he is able to help those who are being tempted" (Heb. 2:17-18). Through faithfulness and prayer, it is possible for a church—regardless of the persecution and worldly influences surrounding it—to "reach unity in the faith and in the knowledge of the Son of God and become mature, attaining to the whole measure of the fullness of Christ" (Eph. 4:13). Paul described this as "work produced by *faith*" (1 Thess. 1:3).

A Powerful Prayer

As a Church, God does not expect us to work out our salvation in our own strength. It is humanly impossible. As Paul reminded the Philippians, "It is God who works in [us]" (Phil. 2:13). That is why Paul prayed so fervently and sincerely for the churches in Asia. He fell to his knees and cried out to God the Father:

> I pray that out of his glorious riches he may strengthen you with power through his Spirit in your inner being, *so that Christ may dwell in your hearts through faith* (Eph. 3:16-17).

Clearly, Paul was not praying for their salvation. They had already been saved "by grace . . . through faith" (Eph. 2:8). Rather, he was praying that their living faith would "grow more and more" (2 Thess. 1:3). Jesus Christ lived in them in the Person of the Holy Spirit, and Paul was praying that they might experience the riches of God's grace. He wanted to see grace and power released in their lives, enabling them to "*walk by faith*" as never before.

Guiding Principles

Principle 1. When measuring a church, we must determine the degree to which doctrinal stability exists in that body.

This quality is not in itself a measure of maturity. In fact, it is possible for people to be doctrinally literate and very well-informed in biblical truth, but to only have head knowledge. What they know about Scripture has not become a part of their lives. On the other hand, it is virtually impossible to live out faith without foundational biblical knowledge. It is important that we know what we believe!

A church that is doctrinally stable

- believes that the Bible is the inspired Word of God;
- believes that salvation is by grace through faith because of the death and resurrection of Jesus Christ;
- believes in the Trinity and understands how God the Father, God the Son and God the Holy Spirit function in the life of the Church;
- believes in the second coming of Jesus Christ.

Without a basic knowledge of *the* faith (what the Bible really teaches), Christians are vulnerable to negative influences from false teachers, and today these false teachers are everywhere. They communicate their message through literature, audiocassettes and videotapes. They are on television and radio. They even go from door to door. Moreover, there are many so-called "Christian churches" that no longer believe in the fundamental truths of Scripture. Immature Christians who come under these influences are open to being "tossed back and forth by the waves, and blown here and there by every wind of teaching" (Eph. 4:14).

Principle 2. When measuring a church, we must determine the degree to which Christians in that body demonstrate that they are God's workmanship, created in Christ Jesus to do good works.

Paul summarized this "work produced by faith" in the following paragraph that he wrote to the Asian churches in his letter to the Ephesians:

> You were taught, with regard to your former way of life, to *put off* your old self, which is being corrupted by its deceitful desires; to be made new in the attitude of your minds; and to *put on* the new self, created to be like God in true righteousness and holiness (4:22-24).

Paul then went on to summarize what this new life in Christ should be like, what they should put on and what they should put off in all of their relationships. Note how these qualities of maturity reflect the same "work produced by faith" we see in both the Thessalonian and Hebrew correspondence:

- HONESTY

Therefore each of you must put off falsehood and speak truthfully to his neighbor (Eph. 4:25).

- SELF-CONTROL

"In your anger do not sin": Do not let the sun go down while you are still angry (Eph. 4:26).

- ETHICAL BEHAVIOR

He who has been stealing must steal no longer (Eph. 4:28).

- GENEROSITY

[He] must work, doing something useful with his own hands, that he may have something to share with those in need (Eph. 4:28).

- WHOLESOME TALK

Do not let any unwholesome talk come out of your mouths, but only what is helpful for building others up according to their needs (Eph. 4:29).

- LACK OF BITTERNESS

Get rid of all bitterness, rage and anger, brawling and slander, along with every form of malice (Eph. 4:31).

- A SPIRIT OF FORGIVENESS

> Be kind and compassionate to one another, forgiving each other, just as in Christ God forgave you (Eph. 4:32).

- MORALITY

> But among you there must not be even a hint of sexual immorality, or of any kind of impurity, or of greed, because these are improper for God's holy people. Nor should there be obscenity, foolish talk or coarse joking, which are out of place, but rather thanksgiving (Eph. 5:3-4).

Principle 3. When measuring a church, we must determine the degree to which Christians are praying that Christ's life will be developed within them.

The essence of Paul's prayer for the Ephesians is that all of them should be "filled to the measure of all the fullness of God" (Eph. 3:19).This fullness will be achieved when believers pray for one another "that Christ may dwell in [our] hearts through faith" (3:17).

Below, I have included a prayer that is a paraphrase of the above passage from Ephesians. This prayer can serve as a wonderful model for every local church. When a church sincerely prays and practices the essence of this prayer, it will begin to experience the riches of God's power that will be released through the Holy Spirit. They will begin to demonstrate a "work produced by faith" and will be talked about throughout the community and beyond. To what extent is your church praying the essence of this prayer and experiencing the results?

For this reason we kneel before You, Father, from whom Your whole family in heaven and on Earth derives its name. We pray that out of Your glorious riches You may strengthen us with power through Your Spirit in our inner being, so that Christ may dwell in our hearts through faith. And we pray that we, being rooted and established in love, may have power, together with all the saints, to grasp how wide and long and high and deep is the love of Christ, and to know this love that surpasses knowledge—that we may be filled to the measure of all the fullness of God.

It is only fitting that we conclude this chapter with Paul's great doxology, which explains and verifies the potential any church has to demonstrate a "work produced by faith":

> Now to him who is able to do immeasurably more than all we ask or imagine, according to his power that is at work within us, to him be glory in the church and in Christ Jesus throughout all generations, for ever and ever! Amen (Eph. 3:20-21).

THINKING AND GROWING TOGETHER

1. What does our church believe about
   - the authority of Scripture?
   - the doctrine of salvation (how we are saved)?
   - God the Father, God the Son and God the Holy Spirit?
   - the second coming of Jesus Christ?

2. What scriptural references and passages can we use to demonstrate that the doctrinal beliefs in our church demontrate the teachings in the Bible?

3. How is our church demonstrating "work produced by faith" (1 Thess. 1:3) as described by Paul in Ephesians 4:25–5:4? Use the following scale from 1 to 10 to evaluate the extent to which your church is manifesting "work produced by faith."

HONESTY

Not at all 1 2 3 4 5 6 7 8 9 10 All the time

SELF-CONTROL

Not at all 1 2 3 4 5 6 7 8 9 10 All the time

ETHICAL BEHAVIOR

Not at all 1 2 3 4 5 6 7 8 9 10 All the time

GENEROSITY

Not at all 1 2 3 4 5 6 7 8 9 10 All the time

WHOLESOME TALK

Not at all 1 2 3 4 5 6 7 8 9 10 All the time

LACK OF BITTERNESS

Not at all 1 2 3 4 5 6 7 8 9 10 All the time

A SPIRIT OF FORGIVENESS

Not at all 1 2 3 4 5 6 7 8 9 10 All the time

MORALITY

Not at all 1 2 3 4 5 6 7 8 9 10 All the time

4. In what creative ways can your church spend time praying Paul's prayer that "Christ may dwell in your hearts through faith" (Eph. 3:17)?

Notes

1. Each of the directives in Ephesians 6:11-17 is stated in the second person plural in the Greek text. In other words, Paul was writing that as a community of faith, we are to stand firm "with the belt of truth," to "take the helmet of salvation," to take "the sword of the Spirit, which is the word of God," etc.
2. A. Skevington Wood, *Ephesians*, vol. 7 of *The Expositors Bible Commentary* (Grand Rapids, MI: Zondervan, 1978), p. 36.

C H A P T E R 7

Hope That Endures

Early in my Christian life, if you had asked me if I was sure I would go to heaven when I died, I would have said, "I hope so!" Sadly, I would have been echoing the total membership of the church I attended at the time. In our theology, no one could know for sure if they were going to "make it" all the way to heaven. To claim certainty would be considered presumptuous, even arrogant.

Fortunately for me, my answer has changed. As I began to study the Scriptures more carefully, I discovered that God wants all of us as His children to be able to respond to any question about our eternal destiny with an "I know so!"—not an "I hope so." This is what biblical *hope* is all about. It is all about God and His grace, not about us and our works. And when we truly understand this wonderful truth, we can only respond with joyful humility.

In English, we often use the word "hope" as a wish or desire, and always with a degree of uncertainty. For example, I may "hope" to take a vacation at some point during the year. I have this hope even though I cannot be absolutely sure it will happen.

By contrast, the term "hope," as it was used by New Testament writers, has an unwavering quality to it and is one of the true measures of a church. The eternal hope we have in Christ is certain and secure. As the author of Hebrews wrote, we can "take hold of the *hope* offered to us [and] be greatly encouraged [because] we have this *hope* as an anchor for the soul, firm and secure" (Heb. 6:18-19).

This does not mean we will never doubt the reality of this hope. In fact, some Christians do not understand it—just as I did not. Even if a Christian does understand it, his or her faith may grow weak. But this does not affect the certainty of our hope. This is why the writer of Hebrews exhorted believers to "hold *unswervingly* to the *hope* we profess" (Heb. 10:23).

The Divine Trilogy

Hope is a part of the divine trilogy that New Testament writers used to measure the maturity level of the local church. And when lack of hope was a weak link in any given body, they addressed this issue. We see this in Paul's writings, especially in Ephesians and 2 Thessalonians.

The Ephesian Correspondence

When Paul wrote this letter to the Ephesians and the other churches in Asia, he did not begin by thanking God for their faith, hope and love as he did when he wrote to the

Thessalonians and to the Colossians. Rather, he began by praising God the Father of our Lord Jesus Christ for all true believers' wonderful blessings and calling in Christ:

> For *he chose us* in him before the creation of the world to be holy and blameless in his sight. In love *he predestined us* to be adopted as his sons through Jesus Christ. . . . In him [Christ] *we have redemption* through his blood, the *forgiveness of sins*, in accordance with the riches of God's grace. . . . Having believed, you were *marked in him with a seal*, the promised Holy Spirit, who is a *deposit guaranteeing our inheritance* until the redemption of those who are God's possession (Eph. 1:4-5,7,13-14).

Paul went on to thank God for two qualities: the *faith* and *love* that existed among these believers. However, he then zoomed in on what was a great spiritual need in their Christian lives:

> I pray also that the eyes of your heart may be enlightened in order that you may know the *hope* to which he has called you (Eph. 1:18).

The Historical Setting

To understand Paul's focus on the need to comprehend and know the *hope* to which God had called these believers, we need to review the religious and cultural background of the people to whom Paul wrote.

On his third missionary journey, Paul returned to Ephesus and established a spiritual beachhead. As he had done in many places where there was a synagogue, he began his ministry among the Jewish people. After three months of intense resistance from those who "refused to believe" (Acts 19:9), he left the synagogue and taught each day in the lecture hall of Tyrannus, where many people made decisions to receive Christ as their Messiah. He continued this ministry "for two years, so that all the Jews and Greeks who lived in the province of Asia heard the word of the Lord" (Acts 19:10).

Many people who came to this great city to do business or to worship in the temple of Artemis (also called Diana) came to hear Paul and became believers. Evidently, they returned to their hometowns where, armed with the gospel message, they started churches. This is why it appears that Paul's letter to the Ephesians was a circular letter to the churches throughout Asia. Paul's frequent references to the universal Church rather than to a particular local church explains his broader purpose.

Also note that *both* Jews and Greeks came from all over Asia and responded to the gospel (see Acts 19:10). As a result, some people who heard this letter read in their churches had come from a God-centered religious background, while others had come from a pagan religious background.

Ethnic Conflicts

Predictably, this cultural and religious mix created some unusual problems in these local churches. There are always difficulties when we attempt to mix people from different social and ethnic backgrounds. However, the predicament intensifies when those mixed communities consist of individuals who represent strong religious cultures that vary greatly in terms of attitudes, values and doctrines.

Such conflicts arose in Ephesus and the other churches in Asia. Because God had definitely chosen Israel to be His people, the Jewish converts evidently believed that they had a special place in the kingdom of God. They had not yet learned the lesson the apostle Peter had to learn when he received a vision from heaven instructing him not to "call anything impure that God has made clean" (Acts 10:15). When Peter entered a

Gentile home in Caesarea and discovered how God had already communicated with Cornelius, he stated: "I *now* realize how true it is that God does not show favoritism but accepts men from every nation who fear him and do what is right" (Acts 10:34-35). If Peter, the leader and main spokesman for the apostles, was still prejudiced and ignorant about God's grace—probably as long as five years after the Church had been born—we can certainly understand why the Jewish people in the province of Asia felt they had a corner on God's grace.

This mentality is to be expected. After all, the children of Israel were given the "covenants of the promise" (Eph. 2:12) when God revealed Himself to Abraham, Isaac and Jacob, and eventually to Moses at Mount Sinai. However, the Gentiles who came to Christ in Ephesus and in the surrounding area were *uncircumcised* pagans. As Paul reminded them, they were "excluded from citizenship in Israel," they were "foreigners to the covenants of the promise," and they were "without hope and without God in the world" (Eph. 2:12) in contrast to their Jewish neighbors who at least had a religious history based on God's Old Testament revelation.

Did this give the believing Jews an advantage? A casual observer might think so. After all, Jesus Himself was Jewish—He was one of them. Furthermore, Paul, the one who brought the message of salvation to this region, was also "of the people of Israel," "a Hebrew of Hebrews" and "of the tribe of Benjamin"; and like all faithful sons of Abraham, he had been "circumcised on the eighth day" (Phil. 3:5; see also Gen. 17:9-14).

In Need of a Savior

Paul wanted all believers (both Jews and Gentiles) who heard this letter read to understand that as a religious Jew, he and his fellow Israelites did not have a special place in the church. "We were by nature objects of wrath," Paul wrote, referring to both Jewish people and Gentiles (Eph. 2:3; see also Rom. 3:23). All people are "dead in . . . transgressions and sins" (Eph. 2:1), regardless of their ethical and religious backgrounds. Everyone needs a Savior and everyone who responds in faith will be saved, by God's grace and not by any works of the law (see Eph. 2:5,8-9). Jesus Christ had come to bring the message of peace to those who "were *far away* [Gentiles] and peace to those *who were near* [Jews]" (Eph. 2:17).

To make sure they really understood that both believing Jews and Gentiles had access to the Father by one Spirit, Paul culminated these thoughts with this reassuring paragraph (note the metaphors Paul used to describe the Church):

> Consequently, you [Gentiles] are no longer foreigners and aliens, but fellow citizens with God's people [the Jews] and members of *God's household* [the church], built on the foundation of the apostles and prophets, with Christ Jesus himself as the chief cornerstone. In him the *whole building* is joined together and rises to become a *holy temple* in the Lord. And in him you too are being built together to become *a dwelling* in which God lives by his Spirit (Eph. 2:19-22).

Only One Body

Paul went on to explain his own unique calling in Christ, which was to be an apostle to the Gentiles in order to preach the "mystery of Christ" (see Eph. 3:2-5). He made it clear that he considered himself to be one with Gentile believers:

> Through the gospel the Gentiles are heirs together with Israel, members together of *one body*, and sharers together in the promise in Christ Jesus (Eph. 3:6).

Being "one body" in Christ is the theme that runs throughout the entire Ephesian letter (see also 1:10; 2:14,16,21-22; 4:4-6,13,16). Paul taught that *all* believers who had this wonderful hope and eternal calling form one body, no matter what their cultural, ethnic or religious backgrounds. Paul was adamant about this when he wrote to the Galatians:

> There is neither Jew nor Greek, slave nor free, male nor female, for you are all one in Christ Jesus (Gal. 3:28).

One Hope

At this point in the letter, Paul clarified why he initially prayed that they might understand the *hope* they have in Christ:

> There is *one body* and one Spirit—just as you were called to *one hope* when you were called—*one Lord, one faith, one baptism; one God and Father of all*, who is over all and through all and in all (Eph. 4:4-6).

Why would Paul urge these believers to work hard at maintaining the oneness they had in Christ? It appears that some of the Jewish believers were demonstrating an element of pride and arrogance in their *calling in Christ* because they had an *earlier calling*, when God called the nation of Israel to be His own special people. They were among "those who were near," not pagan Gentiles who were far away from God (Eph. 2:17). This is why Paul, when using this terminology regarding all Jewish people before they became true believers, went on to write unequivocally:

> For he himself is our peace, who has *made the two one* and has destroyed the barrier, the dividing wall of hostility. His purpose was to create in himself *one new man out of the two*, thus making peace (Eph. 2:14-15).

> For through him we *both* have access to the Father by one Spirit (Eph. 2:18).

This divisive issue in these churches also gives new meaning to Paul's culminating statement in Ephesians:

> From him the *whole body*, joined and held together by *every supporting ligament*, grows and builds itself up in love, as each part does its work (Eph. 4:16).

The Thessalonian Correspondence

As I wrote in chapter 5, when Paul first addressed the Thessalonian believers, he commended them for their "work produced by *faith* . . . labor prompted by *love* . . . [and] endurance inspired by *hope*" (1 Thess. 1:3). However, in his second letter to these same believers, the concept of hope was missing in his opening greeting. He thanked God that their *faith* was "growing more and more" and that their "love . . . for each other [was] increasing" (2 Thess. 1:3). Rather than thanking God for their "endurance inspired by *hope*," as he had in the first letter, Paul omitted this important value. Why didn't he thank God that their hope had also been growing and becoming more stable and steadfast? Paul answered this question in the letter itself.

But this gets us ahead of the story. Let's first reconstruct the history of the Thessalonian church. Against that backdrop, we will clearly discover why, in his second letter, Paul did not commend the Thessalonians for their hope. Furthermore, we will see how he addressed their weakness.

Establishing the Church

Thessalonica was a thriving commercial town located on a trade route in Macedonia. It was here that Paul and his fellow missionaries, Silas and Timothy, proclaimed the gospel and started a church that was destined to become one of the most talked about bodies of believers in Macedonia, and even in the bordering province of Achaia (see 1 Thess. 1:7-8).

The church was born in the midst of persecution. In fact, resentment and oppression became so brutal that Paul and Silas eventually had to leave the city at night because their lives were in danger (see Acts 17:5,10). Nonetheless, in spite of strong opposition, while the missionaries were in Thessalonica they continued to win people to Christ and to diligently and sensitively teach the new converts the basic doctrines of the Christian faith (see 1 Thess. 2:2-6).

Paul beautifully detailed this process in his first letter to that church. Initially they nurtured these new believers "like a mother caring for her little children" (1 Thess. 2:7). As these believers grew in their faith, the missionaries took on a fatherly role. Paul wrote:

> For you know that we dealt with each of you as a father deals with his own children, encouraging, comforting and urging you to live lives worthy of God, who calls you into his kingdom and glory (1 Thess. 2:11-12).

The Second Coming of Christ

During this personal process of discipling, these New Testament missionaries did a masterful job of grounding new believers in the major doctrines of the Christian faith, especially in view of the fact that many of the converts had been committed pagans who had worshiped idols (see 1 Thess. 1:9). During this time, Paul must have concentrated on teaching these new converts about the second coming of Jesus Christ. People throughout Macedonia and Achaia had heard about the Thessalonians' faith in God and how these believers were waiting "for his Son from heaven, whom he raised from the dead—Jesus, who rescues us from the coming wrath" (1 Thess. 1:10).

Later in this same letter, Paul implied that he had carefully gone over many details regarding this doctrine when he wrote:

> Now, brothers, about times and dates we do not need to write to you, for you know very well that the day of the Lord will come like a thief in the night (1 Thess. 5:1-2).

Refreshing their minds, Paul asked them in his second letter, "Don't you remember that when I was with you I used to tell you these things?" (2 Thess. 2:5).

One of the reasons Paul concentrated on teaching these new believers about Christ's second coming certainly related to the severe persecution they faced. The most encouraging words that Paul could give them were that they had *hope* in the midst of these trials. That hope was a prospect of deliverance from this present world, a time in the future when they would be transported into the eternal presence of God.

Satan's Specific Strategy

It appears that Satan chose this doctrinal strength in the Thessalonian church as a target for confusion. This should not surprise us. The enemy of our soul will do anything he can to destroy and weaken a church. If he cannot hit us head on, he will infiltrate. He will come as a roaring lion. If that does not work, then he will appear as an angel of light. If he cannot get to us by attacking our weaknesses, he will undermine our strengths.

From Paul's first Thessalonian letter, we know the believers there handled persecution well. They had grown spiritually in the midst of stress and opposition. Their hope in Christ was steadfast and certain (see 1 Thess. 1:3).

Just when all was going along as expected, something happened! As we read 2 Thessalonians, we discover why Paul omitted any reference to their hope in his initial greeting the second time he writes. Although he was not aware of the specific source of the Thessalonians' doctrinal problem, he knew it involved what they *thought* he had taught.

> [Do not become] alarmed by some prophecy, report or letter supposed to have come from us saying that the day of the Lord has already come (2 Thess. 2:2).

This, of course, explains why Paul commended them for their "growing faith" and their "increasing love," but said nothing about their "endurance inspired by hope." The fact is, they were wavering in their *hope*—as we would if we believed we were facing God's wrath on Earth. Clearly, they had become "unsettled [and] alarmed" (2 Thess. 2:2), which is the opposite of being "steadfast" and "secure," reflecting the "endurance inspired by hope," which they once demonstrated.

Correcting False Doctrine

Paul next began the process of reestablishing the Thessalonians in their hope. "Don't let anyone deceive you in any way," Paul reassured them, "for that day will not come until the rebellion occurs and the man of lawlessness is revealed, the man doomed to destruction" (2 Thess. 2:3).

It is important to understand that a day in Scripture does not necessarily refer to a 24-hour day, but to a period of time. We are now living in the "day of salvation" (2 Cor. 6:2)—and we have been for about 2,000 years. Moreover, there is a period of time coming that is defined as the "day of the Lord" or the "day of God" (2 Pet. 3:12). This day will certainly be initiated at a particular point in time, but it will continue for years, as we calculate time today. At some point after this period begins, God's wrath will be directly poured out on sinful humanity—those who have rejected the gospel. I believe that this period of time will begin after the true universal Church is raptured or taken out of the world (see 1 Cor. 15:51-54), to be followed by a seven-year tribulation period and by the 1,000-year reign of Christ on Earth. If this is a correct interpretation, the "day of the Lord" will then end at the Great White Throne Judgment.

Regardless of whether or not we concur on the specific details, most Christians *do* agree that we are now living in the "day of grace." God has allowed sin in many respects to go unchecked. This is obvious as we look around us, even in our own culture. Many people who are wicked flourish more than those who are Christian. We must understand that God "causes his sun to rise on the evil and the good, and sends rain on the righteous and the unrighteous" (Matt. 5:45). This is the "day of salvation." All people are invited to respond to the grace of God, to receive the Lord Jesus Christ as their personal Savior and to be saved from their sins. The "day of the Lord" has not yet come because God *is* patient. He does not want "anyone to perish, but everyone to come to repentance" (2 Pet. 3:9).

Sometime and in some way between Paul's first and second letters, the Thessalonians were led to believe that this "day" had already begun. Someone evidently posed as Paul's representative and had communicated that they were about to experience God's wrath and judgment on Earth.

Paul's primary goal in his second letter was to correct this false impression and to reestablish them in their *hope* by reassuring them that the day of the Lord had *not* yet come. He then encouraged them to "stand firm" and to "hold to the teachings" that he and his fellow missionaries had "passed on" to them, "whether by word of mouth or by letter" (2 Thess. 2:15).

The Foundation of Hope

The hope true believers have is described throughout the New Testament, particularly in Acts. Jesus Christ came to provide this hope, but we do not encounter this reality in Scripture in all its fullness until after He suffered, died and *rose again*. This is true because our *hope in Christ* is inseparable from *His resurrection*.

The apostle Peter first referred to this hope in his sermon on the Day of Pentecost. Quoting from one of David's messianic psalms, Peter described Christ's own hope and how it related to his own resurrection:

> Therefore my heart is glad and my tongue rejoices; my body also will live in hope, because you will not abandon me to the grave, nor will you let your Holy One see decay (Acts 2:26-27).

As we have seen in Paul's letter to the Ephesians, we have hope because Christ lives. It is because of the Lord's resurrection that we too can claim the promise that someday we will also be raised (see Eph. 1:18-20). Jesus had a new and glorified body following the resurrection—and so shall we.

But there were some people in the Corinthian church who were denying the reality of the resurrection of Christ. Listen to Paul's logic as he addressed this false doctrine:

> For if the dead are not raised, then Christ has not been raised either. And if Christ has not been raised, your faith is futile; you are still in your sins. Then those also who have fallen asleep in Christ are lost. If only for this life we have hope in Christ, we are to be pitied more than all men. But Christ has indeed been raised from the dead, the firstfruits of those who have fallen asleep (1 Cor. 15:16-20).

On three unique occasions, Paul bore witness to the resurrection of Jesus Christ, and in each instance, associated Christ's resurrection with his own personal *hope*.

Before the Sanhedrin

When Paul returned to Jerusalem, he faced a very hostile Jewish community. This once dynamic church had been infiltrated with legalism. Ironically, a group of nonbelieving Jews from the province of Asia saw Paul at the Temple. Earlier, they had seen a Gentile Christian named Trophinus with Paul and had recognized him as an Ephesian, which probably meant that these Jews were also from Ephesus (see Acts 21:27-29). These men were likely well aware of Paul's view regarding oneness in Christ—that both believing Jews and Gentiles were united. It was a message that Paul would have taught in the lecture hall of Tyrannus, even before he wrote his Ephesian letter. Consequently, these Jewish people automatically assumed Paul had taken this Gentile into the temple area that was off limits for all but Jews.

Word quickly spread and a riot erupted. A crowd of angry people dragged Paul outside the Temple gates and attempted to kill him. But a Roman commander intervened (see Acts 21:30-32). Because Paul was fluent in both Greek and Aramaic, he was allowed to speak before the crowd that had attacked him. But when Paul mentioned his calling to be an apostle to the Gentiles, another riot started up among the Jews (see Acts 22:1-22). The Romans, who had military jurisdiction over the region, again took him into custody. But when the Roman commander discovered that Paul was not only a Roman citizen but also Jewish, he had him appear before the Jewish Sanhedrin.

Paul, knowing that some of these religious leaders were Sadducees who denied the resurrection (see Acts 23:8) and that some were Pharisees who firmly believed in the resurrection from the dead, he called out to the Sanhedrin: "My brothers,

I am a Pharisee, the son of a Pharisee. I stand on trial because of my *hope in the resurrection of the dead*" (Acts 23:6).

Paul knew how these men thought and reacted. After all, he was once one of them. His ploy worked! The Pharisees and Sadducees started a heated argument over the resurrection—one of the very issues that caused Paul to be taken into custody in the first place. It was not only his ministry to the Gentiles that provoked the Jews, but also that he testified that he had seen the *living and resurrected Christ* and heard Him speak (see Acts: 17-21; 22:6-8).

Before Felix

Because of threats made upon Paul's life, the Roman commander secretly transferred Paul to Caesarea, the seat of the Roman government in this area of the world. But when Ananias, the high priest, discovered Paul's absence, he and some of the others in Jerusalem and a lawyer named Tertullus traveled to Caesarea and presented Felix, the Roman Governor, with charges against Paul. Again, when given opportunity to speak, Paul focused his own testimony on *hope* as it relates to the resurrection. When Felix gave Paul the opportunity to speak, he said:

> I have the same *hope in God* as these men [the Pharisees], that there will be a *resurrection* of both the righteous and the wicked. . . . It is concerning the *resurrection* of the dead that I am on trial before you today (Acts 24:15,21).

Before Agrippa

Because of local politics and Paul's request to defend himself before Caesar, he was kept in custody in Caesarea. However, eventually he had an opportunity to share his testimony before King Agrippa and his wife, Bernice. Notice once again how Paul referred to his *hope* because of the resurrection:

> And now it is because of *my hope* in what God has promised our fathers that I am on trial today. This is the promise our twelve tribes are *hoping* to see fulfilled as they earnestly serve God day and night. O king, it is because of this *hope* that the Jews are accusing me. Why should any of you consider it incredible that *God raises the dead*? (Acts 26:6-8).

Hope and Our Eternal Destiny

I pointed out earlier that in Paul's letter to the Ephesians our hope in Christ assures us that in God's omniscience we are already seated with Christ in heavenly realms (see Eph. 2:6). However, we are still living on Earth, living out this wonderful calling. Here are some additional biblical statements that describe this hope:

The Hope of Experiencing God's Glory

> Therefore, since we have been justified through faith, we have peace with God through our Lord Jesus Christ, through whom we have gained access by faith into this grace in which we now stand. And we rejoice in the *hope of the glory of God* (Rom. 5:1-2).

> God has chosen to make known among the Gentiles the glorious riches of this mystery, which is Christ in you, the *hope of glory* (Col. 1:27).

The Hope of Salvation

> But since we belong to the day, let us be self-controlled, putting on *faith* and *love* as a breastplate, and the *hope of salvation* as a helmet (1 Thess. 5:8).

The Hope of Eternal Life

> So that, having been justified by his grace, we might become heirs having the *hope of eternal life* (Titus 3:7).

A Living Hope

> Praise be to the God and Father of our Lord Jesus Christ! In his great mercy he has given us new birth into a *living hope through the resurrection of Jesus Christ from the dead*, and into an inheritance that can never perish, spoil or fade—kept in heaven for you (1 Pet. 1:3-4).

Hope Reflects Joy

Joy is perhaps one of the most visible evidences of hope in a mature body of Christians. Three times in his letter to the Romans Paul referred to the relationship between *hope* and *joy*:

> We *rejoice* in the *hope* of the glory of God (Rom. 5:2).

> Be *joyful* in *hope* (Rom. 12:12).

> May the God of *hope* fill you with all *joy* and peace as you trust in him, so that you may overflow with *hope* by the power of the Holy Spirit (Rom. 15:13).

In some respects, having the joy that comes from genuine hope is a paradoxical experience. How can Christians rejoice in the midst of persecution and suffering? The answer lies in the hope these believers have even though their lives are being threatened by those who oppose the gospel.

One of the most inspiring stories that has touched my own life is that of Kefa Sempangi, a man who had been pastor of the

14,000-member Redeemed Church in Uganda when Edi Amin held control of this country as a ruthless dictator. Kefa and his family miraculously escaped death and fled to America where I had the privilege of meeting him and then reading his book *A Distant Grief*.[1]

From the very beginning of Amin's reign of terror, his primary target was the Christian Church. In telling his story, Kefa shares one remarkable and miraculous event regarding the way believers in Uganda faced their persecutors.

It was Easter morning 1973. More than 7,000 people had gathered from miles around. After ministering to these people most of the day, Kefa pushed his way through the crowd and finally arrived at the place where he was staying. He quickly noticed that several men had entered his room and had closed the door behind them. They were Amin's assassins.

The tallest of the men pointed his rifle in Kefa's face and told him that they were going to kill him. However, he was going to allow Kefa to share some final words.

Kefa could only stare at this man in shock and unbelief. Fear gripped his soul. But suddenly, he regained his composure and uttered words that could only have come from God's supernatural guidance:

> I do not need to plead my own cause. I'm a dead man already. My life is dead and hidden in Christ. It is your lives that are in danger. You are dead in your sins. I will pray to God that after you have killed me, He will spare you from eternal destruction.[2]

Suddenly, the hatred in these men's faces changed to curiosity. The leader directed them to drop their rifles and they asked Kefa if he would pray for them—right then. Amazed and bewildered, Kefa began to pray for their eternal salvation.

When Kefa completed what was a very simple and direct prayer, Amin's men turned to leave, assuring him of their protection. In fact, these men later became believers and eventually assisted Kefa and his family in their escape from Uganda.

That evening as Kefa drove home, he was deeply puzzled but had joy in his heart. He felt that he had passed from death to life and that he now understood Paul's words to the Galatians:

> I have been crucified with Christ and I no longer live, but Christ lives in me. The life I live in the body, I live by faith in the Son of God, who loved me and gave himself for me (Gal. 2:20).

What motivates followers of Jesus Christ to face this kind of oppression so triumphantly? The answer focuses on a believer's eternal hope in Jesus Christ. This is what motivated Paul to write to the Philippians from a Roman prison, "For to me, to live is Christ and to die is gain" (Phil. 1:21). He knew that if a Roman soldier ended his mortal life, he still had eternal life—a supernatural life—in heaven. "Now we know," he wrote to the Corinthians, "that if the earthly tent we live in is destroyed, we have a building from God, an eternal house in heaven, not built by human hands" (2 Cor. 5:1).

Guiding Principles

Principle 1. When measuring a church, we must look for a full understanding of hope that is based on belief in a literal resurrection of Jesus Christ.

When Paul wrote his first letter to the Thessalonians, he addressed another point of confusion regarding their hope in Christ. Some were confused about their loved ones who had died before Christ's imminent return. Paul reassured them with these wonderful words:

> Brothers, we do not want you to be ignorant about those who fall asleep, or to grieve like of rest of men, who *have no hope*. We believe that *Jesus died and rose again* and so we believe that God will bring with Jesus those who have fallen asleep in him. According to the Lord's own word, we tell you that we who are still alive, who are left till the coming of the Lord, will certainly not precede those who have fallen asleep. For the Lord himself will come down from heaven, with a loud command, with the voice of the archangel and with the trumpet call of God, and the *dead in Christ will rise first.* After that, we who are still alive and are left will be caught up together with them in the clouds to meet the Lord in the air. And so we will be with the Lord forever. Therefore *encourage each other with these words* (1 Thess. 4:13-18).

Principle 2. When measuring a church, we must look for a full understanding of hope that assures all true believers in the Lord Jesus Christ that they have eternal life regardless of their ethnic or religious backgrounds.

What I described at the beginning of this chapter about my own experience illustrates the corporate life of the whole church I grew up in. In fact, if you asked individual members whether or not they knew for sure that they were saved, most of them would never say they had the assurance of their salvation—they could only wait and see! If they obeyed the rules of the church, they might have a chance to enter heaven.

Even though I was a young believer and still confused about the biblical concept of hope, I knew something was desperately wrong with this scene. Sadly, this attitude reflected the corporate beliefs of many of the members of this church.

I remember attending a funeral of a long-time member of this church. Unfortunately, he did not have the greatest reputation in the community or among his family and friends outside the church. Yet he was a staunch believer in the theology of this religious community.

I will never forget the essence of the message that was given that day by one of the local ministers. He offered little hope to the family. He implied that perhaps this man might be allowed to enter heaven–after all, he meant well in spite of his failure to live up to God's standards.

The results of that message were devastating. There was literally weeping and wailing as his family, relatives and friends passed by the casket for a final viewing. The reason for this uncertainty and confusion is easily explained. These professing Christians did not understand the concept of true biblical hope. They desperately needed to understand and believe what the apostle John wrote in his first epistle:

> I write these things to you who believe in the name of the Son of God so that you may know that you have eternal life (1 John 5:13).

It is true that some sincere and able Christian theologians disagree as to whether Christians can ever lose their salvation. However, most serious students of the Bible *agree* that God wants us to be certain every moment of every day that *we are saved*. Furthermore, that security is not based on our works, but on our faith in Christ's death and His Resurrection.

Principle 3. When measuring a church, we must look for a true and full understanding of hope that reflects steadfastness and endurance, no matter what life's circumstances.

Most of us will never face the persecution that the first-century Christians experienced. And most of us in America will not have to face assassins such as the ones my friend Kefa Sempangi encountered when he was a pastor in Uganda. However, each one of us *does* face unsettling challenges, including the unexpected natural catastrophes in life. When we face

---

When measuring a church, we must look for a true and full understanding of hope that reflects steadfastness and endurance.

---

these traumatic moments, if we have true hope in Christ we can experience a sense of peace, even in the midst of very difficult trials and tribulations. As a pastor, I have seen this verified many times over the years. In fact, sometimes I have wondered whether I would have the same measure of strength if I encountered the same difficulties some members of my church have faced! It is at this point, I can only trust God—that He will provide His grace and encouragement in difficult and threatening situations.

One day I talked to a very close friend who had just learned that he had a cancerous brain tumor. The prognosis was not good. In fact, he knew he might die on the operating table. However, I sensed in this man an incredible trust in God. If it was the will of God, he was ready to face death, knowing he would awaken in the presence of God. That is hope!

THINKING AND GROWING TOGETHER

1. Why is a belief in the literal resurrection of Christ a foundational doctrine in measuring the degree the church reflects hope?
2. Why is it that some Christians lack the assurance of their salvation? To what extent does your church reflect "hope of eternal life"?
3. Share some examples of situations in which you have seen Christians reflect steadfastness and endurance in spite of some very difficult circumstances in their lives.
4. Why do some Christians demonstrate so much uncertainty in their lives when value changes take place in our society? What does this say about their hope in Christ?

Notes

1. Kefa Sempangi with Barbara R. Thompson, *A Distant Grief* (Glendale, CA: Regal Books, 1979), n.p.
2. Ibid.

CHAPTER 8

LOVE—THE GREATEST OF THESE

As we have already discovered in this study, the apostle Paul often mentioned the qualities of faith, hope and love when evaluating the maturity level of a church. However, he made it very clear that love is the most important quality of the three.

In this divine trilogy, why is love *the greatest of these* (see 1 Cor. 13:13)? Why not faith or hope? It is easy to be simplistic when answering theological questions. However, in this instance, there is a very succinct but profound answer. Love is greater because this mark of maturity is related to the very essence of who God is. As John stated, "God is love" (1 John 4:8,16).

This certainly does not mean that our creator is some immaterial force called love, or some eternal principal that is operating in our universe. This is a common idea in various religions, but it is not a biblical concept. Rather, to state that "God is love" means that the essential nature of God–the living, personal God–is love. As He is light (see 1 John 1:5) and spirit (see John 4:24), He is also love. Furthermore, the most glorious truth that permeates the New Testament message is that the Lord Jesus Christ became the perfect embodiment of God's eternal love for all mankind (see 1 John 4:9-10).

Of course, we must view faith, hope and love as interrelated virtues when measuring a church. Whereas faith and hope are foundational qualities, love is all encompassing. When a local church practices love as God intended, it demonstrates the most essential doctrine of true Christianity, the Incarnation, "that God was reconciling the world to himself in Christ" (2 Cor. 5:19).

The apostle John expressed this idea in a profound way in the introduction to his Gospel:

> In the beginning was the Word, and the Word was with God, and the Word was God. He was with God in the beginning. The Word became flesh and made his dwelling among us. We have seen his glory, the glory of the One and Only, who came from the Father, full of grace and truth (John 1:1-2,14).

A Quest for Power and Position

To understand why it is so important that we "live a life of love, just as Christ loved us" (Eph. 5:2), we need to go back to that unforgettable scene in the Upper Room in Jerusalem where Jesus met with the apostles shortly before His death. In many respects, what happened there laid the groundwork for building local communities of faith that would spring up all over the Roman world. In fact, the apostles' love for one another was to be a prototype for what God intended every local church to be.

We must remember that Jesus had spent more than three years with these men, teaching them who He was and why He had come into this world. But at this juncture, they still had very little comprehension of God's redemptive plan—without this understanding, they had virtually no insight regarding the part they would play in carrying this message to the world. Even though Jesus had told them clearly, "I will build my church [*ekklesia*]," (Matt. 16:18) they had no clue as to what He really meant. They would have interpreted the term *ekklesia* through their own religious and cultural grid and envisioned Jesus as the future king of Israel, setting them free from pagan authority, such as had been imposed upon them by the Roman Empire.

In the Roman world, the word "*ekklesia*" was used to refer to a large gathering of people, such as the assembly (*ekklesia*) that came together in Ephesus to condemn Paul for his missionary activities (see Acts 19:32). However, the word was also used to refer to an authoritative body, which in Ephesus was the legal assembly (*ekklesia*) that eventually took control of the situation (Acts 19:39).

Certainly, in the context of Jewish culture, the apostles would think of the Sanhedrin as an *ekklesia*—the Sanhedrin was an assembly of 70 men that powerfully controlled both the religious and political life in Israel. The Sanhedrin literally had authority over life and death (see Acts 6:12—8:1). When Jesus said to His men that He would "build his [*ekklesia*]," in their minds Jesus would be the King and they would be His "cabinet members." Though we are not told how often they argued among themselves "as to which of them would be the greatest," we can assume it happened frequently (see Luke 9:46; Mark 9:33). Ironically, James and John went further than any of the other apostles in their quest for position and power. They, along with their mother, asked Jesus if they could sit on His right and left hand in the Kingdom (see Matt. 20:20-21; Mark 10:35-37).

Clearly, all of these men were excited about the potential inherent in their new roles. In their humanness, they became enamored with Jesus' ability to work miracles, and when He occasionally shared these powers with them, they at times abused the privilege. In fact, on one occasion, James and John wanted to call down fire from heaven to destroy some Samaritans because they would not welcome Jesus into their village (see Luke 9:51-54). Jesus had to rebuke James and John for their arrogance and immaturity.

It is difficult to believe that this kind of self-centered behavior occurred a relatively short time before Jesus met with these men to celebrate the Passover meal, the final time before He died as the Lamb of God. In fact, even while they were engaging in this Jewish meal of remembrance, they had another argument about their positions in Christ's kingdom (see Luke 22:24). James and John were probably square in the middle of the squabble, perhaps precipitating it.

Ironically, it was in this shameful context of carnality that Jesus set the stage for teaching them what Paul later identified as "the greatest of these" (1 Cor. 13:13). Not only did the apostles have little understanding regarding faith and hope, they had no comprehension of what Christ was about to do for them and the whole world—*to redeem us from our sins*—the greatest act of love known in the universe.

Of the 12 men Jesus chose to follow Him, the apostle John has recorded the most about this kind of true love. As was previously noted, he and his brother James probably violated the real meaning of agape (love) the most. But just as Jesus chose a materialist like Matthew to record the most about being nonmaterialistic (see Matt. 6:1-34), He also chose a once self-centered and sinful man such as John to record the most about the true meaning of love.

Under the inspiration of the Holy Spirit, John recorded in his Gospel some powerful statements by Jesus that are omitted by Matthew, Mark and Luke. Three times Jesus exhorted the apostles—and us—to "love one another."

A New Command

Jesus' first statement contrasted the law of Moses with a new law—the law of love.

> A new command I give you: Love one another (John 13:34).

All of these men of Galilee clearly understood the law of Moses. But they had totally missed the meaning of another statement Jesus had shared in their presence—probably many times—as He conversed with Jewish religious leaders. He had come to fulfill the law of Moses (see Matt. 5:17) and in so doing, He introduced a new law: *the law of love.*

The apostle Paul, who as a religious Pharisee had initially defended the law of Moses as the means of righteousness, understood this new law after he met Jesus Christ face-to-face on the road to Damascus. Look closely at the words he wrote to the Romans:

> Let no debt remain outstanding, except the continuing debt to *love one another*, for he who loves his fellowman has *fulfilled the law*. The commandments, "Do not commit adultery," "Do not murder," "Do not steal," "Do not covet," and whatever other commandment there may be, are summed up in this one rule: "*Love your neighbor as yourself.*" Love does no harm to its neighbor. *Therefore love is the fulfillment of the law* (Rom. 13:8-10; see also Gal. 5:14).

As I Have Loved You

That evening in the Upper Room, Jesus' words about this "new command" would have meant nothing apart from what these men had just experienced. As I have already noted, at some point during this meal, they had once again begun arguing as to who was the greatest among them (see Luke 22:24). Imagine the emotional pain and disappointment Jesus must have felt in His human spirit! After all, He had spent nearly three years preparing them for this mission.

But this was also the moment Jesus had been waiting for. He took this unique opportunity to teach them a powerful lesson:

> The kings of the Gentiles lord it over them; and those who exercise authority over them call themselves Benefactors. But you are not to be like that. Instead, the greatest among you should be like the youngest, and the one who rules like the one who serves (Luke 22:25-26).

After delivering this pointed message, Jesus quietly got up and began to wash their feet. It had to be a very embarrassing moment, especially since these men knew about the custom. The bowl and towel had been there, but for some reason there was no servant. Knowing all of this, not one of them had volunteered to take on this menial task.

Years later when John wrote his Gospel, he described this scene by saying that "Jesus knew that the time had come for him to leave this world and go to the Father" (John 13:1). He had loved these men all along, but now He "showed them the full extent of his love" (John 13:1). In the midst of this meal, and while they were arguing, Jesus became the servant and began to wash their feet.

Following what was certainly an awkward experience for the apostles, Jesus added to their chagrin by asking them a very pointed question, and then in the same breath answering the question with another powerful lesson:

> "Do you understand what I have done for you?" he asked them. "You call me 'Teacher' and 'Lord,' and rightly so, for that is what I am. Now that I, your Lord and Teacher, have washed your feet, you also should wash one another's feet. I have set you an example that you should do as I have done for you" (John 13:12-15).

Jesus then drove home His point with His second command:

> As I have loved you, so you must love one another (John 13:34).

When Jesus washed the apostles' feet, it was a simple, human act of love to illustrate the supreme act of love He would share with the whole world when He gave His life on the Cross. Ironically, John, who needed this lesson perhaps more

---

When Jesus washed the apostles' feet, it was a simple, human act of love to illustrate the supreme act of love He would share with the whole world when He gave His life on the Cross.

---

than the others, described the full extent of Christ's love in his first epistle. Writing to local churches nearly 50 years after the Last Supper, John was certainly reflecting on this incredible experience. Though he missed the point then, he had since learned the true meaning of that dramatic moment:

> This is how we know what love is: Jesus Christ laid down his life for us. And we ought to lay down our lives for our brothers (1 John 3:16).

This, of course, is what Jesus actually meant when He told them years before, "As I have loved you, so you must love one another" (John 13:34). This was "the *full* extent of his love" (John 13:1). However, at the Last Supper, if Jesus had referred to His sacrificial death, it would have gone in one ear and out the other. After all, the apostles were arguing among themselves who was to be the greatest and were even unwilling to wash one another's feet—or their Master's. Laying down their lives for one another in death would have been a concept so foreign to them they would not have heard the words, let alone have understood this kind of sacrificial love.

Ironically, James, John's brother, was one of the first to demonstrate this ultimate act of love. Early in the history of the church in Jerusalem, he literally gave his life as a martyr for the cause of Christ and his fellow believers (see Acts 12:1-2). James was a man who had been totally transformed by the message of the Cross—a man who had previously wanted power and prestige in Christ's earthly kingdom. What a contrast! Unwilling to wash anyone else's feet at the Passover meal, within a relatively short period of time after the Church was born on the Day of Pentecost, James literally laid down his life for his brothers, a sacrificial act that certainly illustrates why *love* is "the greatest of these."

All Men Will Know

Jesus' next declaration teaches even more specifically why love is "the greatest of these," even more important than our faith and hope. He spoke of His ultimate purpose in coming into this world:

> By this all men will know that you are my disciples, if you love one another (John 13:35).

There were many disciples in Jesus' day, and there were many teachers. But Jesus was no ordinary teacher, and the apostles were not just another group of disciples. Jesus was the God-man–the Word who became flesh. If these men loved each other as Jesus loved them, they would convince unbelievers that they had not only learned great truths from their teacher but that they had also been transformed because of their personal relationship with Jesus Christ, who was the eternal Son of God.

In his Gospel, and prior to his account of the foot-washing experience, John reminded his readers that Jesus had demonstrated that He was indeed the Son of God when He performed miraculous signs. He changed water to wine in Cana (see John 2:1-11), healed the nobleman's son in Capernaum (see John 4:43-54) and healed the impotent man at the pool in Jerusalem (see John 5:1-13). In a wilderness area, He fed 5,000 men and their families "with five small barley loaves and two small fish" (John 6:9). He then walked on the water in the midst of a storm on the Sea of Galilee (see John 6:16-21). Returning to Jerusalem, He healed a man who had been blind from birth (see John 9:1-41). And He culminated His miracle-working power in Bethany by raising Lazarus from the dead (see John 11:1-44). John recorded these seven miraculous signs to convince all of us that Jesus Christ is indeed the Son of God, that we might believe in Him and be saved (see John 20:30-31).

But now Jesus was leaving the awesome task of sharing the message of who He really is with these men. How would they be able to verify and communicate the deity of Christ? When He returned to heaven, at least some of the apostles were able to perform miraculous signs in order to convince people that Jesus was the Son of God and the Savior of the world (see Acts 2:43;

Heb. 2:2-4). But Jesus had a greater sign in mind that evening in the Upper Room, a supernatural and powerful miracle that could continue for centuries in the context of every local church—a miracle that includes every true believer in Christ. Years later, John described this unique miracle in his first epistle:

> Dear friends, since God so loved us, we also ought to *love one another. No one has ever seen God*; but if we *love one another, God lives in us* and his love is made complete in us (1 John 4:11-12).

Once Jesus had returned to the Father, God's ultimate and ongoing miraculous plan was that people would be convinced of who Jesus really is by seeing His deity and righteous life fleshed out in our relationships with one another in our local churches. Jesus wanted these men, and us, to know that this will happen when we truly "love one another." And when we do, they will know we are Jesus' disciples—brothers and sisters in Christ who have been transformed by faith in the Son of God. And as we'll see, this is what Jesus prayed for!

True Love Reflects Righteousness

At some point, Jesus left the Upper Room and with the apostles, headed toward the Garden of Gethsemane. Prior to descending into the Kidron Valley, they must have passed a vineyard. They may have seen the remains of a fire flickering in the darkness, evidence of smoldering coals where the gardener had burned dead branches he had trimmed from the main vine.

Jesus turned this rather common event into another dramatic experience for the apostles in order to teach them the same lesson He had taught them in the Upper Room. However, He took them to a much deeper level to help them understand why love is "the greatest of these" (1 Cor. 13:13).

No doubt pointing to the freshly trimmed branches in the vineyard, He identified Himself as the "true vine" and God the Father as "the gardener" (John 15:1). In this metaphor, the apostles were the "branches" (John 15:5).

Judas had already left the scene in order to betray Jesus, and his absence was a significant part of the lesson Jesus was teaching the others. Sadly, Judas was like a "branch" that a gardener "cuts off" and is then "thrown into the fire and burned" (John 15:2,6). However, the rest of these men were not "dead branches." They were beginning to "bear fruit" (John 15:2), although it had been almost nonexistent. Consequently, each of them was like a branch the gardener "prunes so that it will be even more fruitful" (John 15:2). In other words, Jesus had been "pruning" these men as He taught them their greatest lesson in humility when He washed their feet. And, if all of them continued to draw their strength from Jesus Christ–the true vine–they would eventually "bear much fruit" (John 15:5).

Jesus then culminated this dramatic lesson with a statement that was very similar to the one He had shared with them in the Upper Room:

> This is to my Father's glory, that you bear much fruit, showing yourselves to be my disciples (John 15:8; compare with 13:34).

There are various opinions as to what this fruit really is. However, it seems clear that what Jesus shared earlier in the Upper Room and what He said at this moment answers this question. The fruit is a demonstration of Christ's love in the apostles lives–a love that would show unbelievers that they were Jesus' disciples. Carefully read the paragraph that follows this remarkable event:

> As the Father has loved me, so have I loved you. Now *remain in my love.* If you obey my commands, you will *remain in my love*, just as I have obeyed my Father's commands and *remain in his love.* My command is this: *Love each other* as I have loved you. Greater love has no one than this, that he lay down his life for his friends. You are my friends if you do what I command. You did not choose me, but I chose you and appointed you to go and bear fruit—fruit that will last. Then the Father will give you whatever you ask in my name. This is my command: *Love each other* (John 15:9-10,12-14,16-17).

With this vivid illustration, Jesus introduced His disciples to an even deeper dimension of love. It was a new depth of love that goes beyond just serving one another, which Jesus had modeled with the foot-washing episode. This deeper dimension is the "fruit of righteousness," which is the focus of Paul's prayer for the Philippian Christians:

> And this is my prayer: that your love may abound more and more in knowledge and depth of insight, so that you may be able to discern what is best and may be pure and blameless until the day of Christ, filled with the fruit of righteousness that comes through Jesus Christ—to the glory and praise of God (Phil. 1:9-11).

Paul underscored this same truth in his letter to the Ephesians. After exhorting these believers to "live a life of love, just as Christ loved us" (Eph. 5:2), he contrasted the kingdom of light with the kingdom of darkness:

> For you were once darkness, but now are you light in the Lord. Live as children of light (for the fruit of the light

> consists in all goodness, righteousness and truth) and find out what pleases the Lord. Have nothing to do with the fruitless deeds of darkness, but rather expose them (Eph. 5:8-11).

True Love Reflects Unity

The next major event in this unique sequence involves Jesus' prayer as He and His 11 disciples continued their journey toward the Garden of Gethsemane. Jesus "looked toward heaven" and uttered these remarkable words:

> My prayer is not for them alone [the eleven]. I pray also for those who will believe in me through their message [all believers], that all of them may be one, Father, just as you are in me and I am in you. May they also be in us so *that the world may believe that you have sent me.* I have given them the glory that you gave me, that they may be one as we are one: I in them and you in me. *May they be brought to complete unity to let the world know that you sent me* and have loved them even as you have loved me (John 17:20-23).

Jesus' statement in the Upper Room exhorting His followers to "love one another" (John 13:34), plus the meaning of the metaphor involving the vine and the branches bearing "much fruit" (John 15:5), gives a wondrous meaning to His prayer for the apostles and for all of us who have come to faith in Christ because of their ministry. We can now understand more fully why love is "the greatest of these" (1 Cor. 13:13). Before Jesus told these men to "make disciples" (Matt. 28:19), He wanted the world to be able to see true, dedicated disciples. In essence, we are to reflect who Jesus Christ really is by serving "one another in love" (Gal. 5:13) and reflecting Christ's righteousness in all our relationships, which Paul calls "the fruit of the Spirit" (Gal.

5:22-23). This kind of Christlike love in turn creates unity and oneness in our churches that reveals to the world the unity and oneness that exists in the eternal community itself: the Father, Son and Holy Spirit. Agape love is "the greatest of these" because in a magnificent and miraculous way, it demonstrates that God was in Christ reconciling the world to Himself and then indwelling all of us in the person of the Holy Spirit to enable us to indeed "live a life of love, just as Christ loved us."

Jesus' New Commandment and the New Testament Letters

Jesus' new commandment that John recorded and illustrated in his Gospel set the stage for what God intended the Church to be—a caring and holy community of love that demonstrates the essence of the Gospel, which theologians call the great *kenosis.* This word means "emptying" and describes what Christ did when He came into this world. Paul recorded this process in his letter to the Philippians. When Jesus Christ was "in very nature God, [he] did not consider equality with God something to be grasped, but [He] made himself nothing [and took on Himself] the very nature of a servant. [He was] made in human likeness [and then] humbled himself and became obedient to death—even death on a cross" (Phil. 2:6-8).

What Jesus did is indeed the essence of our message to the world. And when we love others as Christ loved us, we miraculously visualize and verify the reality of this message. In other words, our love for one another is the ultimate measure of a church.

This is why we repeatedly encounter Christ's new commandment in the letters that were written to first-century churches. In fact, the directives and exhortations to love others appear approximately 50 times in the epistles. Here are some of these injunctions which certainly help explain what Jesus had in mind when He said, "Love one another":

- If you really keep the royal law found in Scripture, "Love your neighbor as yourself," you are doing right (Jas. 2:8; see also Gal. 5:14).

- But do not use your freedom to indulge the sinful nature; rather, serve one another in love (Gal. 5:13).

- And in fact, you do love all the brothers throughout Macedonia. Yet we urge you, brothers, to do so more and more (1 Thess. 4:10).

- Do everything in love (1 Cor. 16:14).

- Be completely humble and gentle; be patient, bearing with one another in love (Eph. 4:2).

- Instead, speaking the truth in love, we will in all things grow up into him who is the Head, that is, Christ (Eph. 4:15).

- Live a life of love, just as Christ loved us and gave himself up for us as a fragrant offering and sacrifice to God (Eph. 5:2).

- Husbands, love your wives, just as Christ loved the church and gave himself up for her (Eph. 5:25; see also Eph. 5:28; 5:33; Col. 3:19).

- Then make my joy complete by being like-minded, having the same love, being one in spirit and purpose (Phil. 2:2).

- And over all these virtues put on love, which binds them all together in perfect unity (Col. 3:14).

- The goal of this command is love, which comes from a pure heart and a good conscience and a sincere faith (1 Tim. 1:5).
- Set an example for the believers in speech, in life, in love, in faith and in purity (1 Tim. 4:12).
- Pursue righteousness, godliness, faith, love, endurance and gentleness (1 Tim. 6:11; see also 2 Tim. 2:22).
- Teach the older men to be . . . sound in faith, in love and in endurance (Titus 2:2).
- Train the younger women to love their husbands and children (Titus 2:4).
- And let us consider how we may spur one another on toward love and good deeds (Heb. 10:24).
- Now that you have purified yourselves by obeying the truth so that you have sincere love for your brothers, love one another deeply, from the heart (1 Pet. 1:22).
- Show proper respect to everyone: Love the brotherhood of believers, fear God, honor the king (1 Pet. 2:17).
- Live in harmony with one another; be sympathetic, love as brothers, be compassionate and humble (1 Pet. 3:8).
- Above all, love each other deeply, because love covers over a multitude of sins (1 Pet. 4:8).
- This is the message you heard from the beginning: We

should love one another (1 John 3:11).

- We know that we have passed from death to life, because we love our brothers (1 John 3:14).

- Dear children, let us not love with words or tongue but with actions and in truth (1 John 3:18).

- And this is his command: to believe in the name of his Son, Jesus Christ, and to love one another as he commanded us (1 John 3:23).

- Dear friends, let us love one another, for love comes from God (1 John 4:7).

- Dear friends, since God so loved us, we also ought to love one another (1 John 4:11).

- And he has given us this command: Whoever loves God must also love his brother (1 John 4:21).

- This is how we know that we love the children of God: by loving God and carrying out his commands (1 John 5:2).

- I ask that we love one another (2 John 5).

- As you have heard from the beginning, his command is that you walk in love (2 John 6).

What is Biblical Love?

As I have already written, the apostle John, who shared more about biblical love than any other New Testament writer, has given us the ultimate definition of love.

> This is how we know what love is: Jesus Christ laid down his life for us. And we ought to lay down our lives for our brothers (1 John 3:16).

However, few of us are called upon to do what John's brother James did as well as some of the other apostles, to literally die so that others might hear the gospel. Consequently, how does this definition of love apply to our day-to-day tasks and relationships? How is our love measured in our local, life-on-life communities of faith?

As we have already seen in chapter 5, Paul defined love by illustrating what was lacking in the Corinthian church. Because Paul referred to love as "the greatest of these" in this letter to these very immature believers, let's review Paul's profile.

Henry Drummond, in his classic little book titled *The Greatest Thing in the World*, describes the qualitites Paul outlined in 1 Corinthians 13:4-6 as the "spectrum of love." He then breaks this "spectrum" into nine qualities:

1. patience (Love is patient.)
2. kindness (Love is kind.)
3. generosity (It does not envy.)
4. humility (It does not boast, it is not proud.)
5. courtesy (It is not rude.)
6. unselfishness (It is not self-seeking.)
7. good-temper (It is not easily angered.)
8. guilelessness (It keeps no records of wrongs.)
9. sincerity (Love does not delight in evil but rejoices with the truth.)[1]

It is important to understand that these qualities are primarily attitudes and actions, not feelings. For example:

- We have the opportunity to demonstrate *patience* when we are frustrated and even have angry feelings.

- *Kindness* is an act of the will that may or may not be generated by positive feelings.

- *Generosity* may involve actions that make us uncomfortable, especially if it means responding to others needs in a sacrificial manner.

- *Humility* involves considering others better than ourselves, not just looking to our own interests (see Phil. 2:3-4).

- *Being courteous* may involve "turning the other cheek" when someone irritates us or even hurts us.

- *Unselfishness* may not come easily, especially when we feel someone else is actually responding selfishly to us—or to someone else.

- Facing *anger* in others usually doesn't make it easy for us to maintain a *good temper*.

- To be *guileless*—to keep our own motives pure—is always difficult when we are forced into a situation in which others are resorting to deception in order to come out on top.

- Sincerely rejoicing when good things happen to others when those same good things do not happen to us is always difficult—but it's a true test of love!

The Corinthians lacked most of these qualities (see chapter 5). Though they had received more spiritual gifts than any other church, they were impatient with one another. Divisions permeated the church. Their impatience reflected itself in unkind acts. They violated the quality of generosity because of their envy. They certainly were not humble—they were prideful and puffed up. Even in their communion meals, they demonstrated selfishness, gluttony and drunkenness. Selfishness and guile permeated their

---

Though faith and hope are foundational in measuring up to the fullness of Christ, the ultimate and most important quality is love.

---

business lives as they sued each other in pagan courts. And, of course, lingering anger was a part of this process. They were deceptive and deceitful, attempting to take advantage of each other. Now how could they be sincere when they were actually rejoicing in the immorality that existed in the church?

The Corinthians' imperfections stated positively become a rather comprehensive definition of true biblical love. Paul identified this spectrum as "the greatest of these" (1 Cor. 13:13). Though *faith* and *hope* are foundational in measuring up to the fullness of Christ, the ultimate and most important quality is *love*. "By this," Jesus said to His disciples, "all men will know that you are my disciples, if you *love one another*" (John 13:35).

Love and the Functioning Body

There is a direct correlation between expressing true biblical love in the church and the way the church becomes mature. Paul affirmed this when he said that the Body of Christ "builds itself up in love, as each part does its work" (Eph. 4:16).

This raises a very important question. How does God intend for each member of a local church to function in order for the Church to become a loving and unified community? When I first began to study the biblical truths outlined in this book on how to measure a church, I noticed a major concept that kept jumping off the pages of the New Testament letters. Again and again I noticed exhortations regarding what believers are *to do for one another*. In fact, Paul used the Greek word "*allelon*" ("one another") nearly 40 times to instruct Christians regarding their mutual responsibilities to their fellow believers.

As I studied this idea in Scripture, I saw this as a very important key in helping a local church grow and build itself up in love. Once I began to teach and emphasize the one-another injunctions, I saw it impact other churches, too.

Not surprising, the injunction that is emphasized the most is that we are to love one another, or each other (see John 13:34-35; Rom. 13:8; 1 Thess. 3:12; 4:9; 2 Thess. 1:3; Heb. 10:24; 1 Pet. 1:22; 1 John 3:11, 23; 1 John 4:7,11-12; 2 John 5). As we have seen in this chapter, this love is a foundational concept. It is both the process and the goal. The process is to love one another as Christ loved us on an ongoing basis and the goal is to reflect God's love in our relationships with one another.

In order to love one another, the epistles give us a number of directives that will enable us to carry out this process. Here is a list of what I call one-another injunctions.

We are to confess sins to one another (see Jas. 5:16).
We are to pray for one another (see Jas. 5:16).
We are to serve one another (see Gal. 5:13).
We are to carry one another's burdens (see Gal. 6:2).

We are to encourage one another (see 1 Thess. 4:18; 5:11,14).
We are to wait for one another (see 1 Cor. 11:33).
We are to care for one another (see 1 Cor. 12:25).
We are to function as members of one another (see Rom. 12:5).
We are to be devoted to one another (see Rom. 12:10).
We are to honor one another (see Rom. 12:10).
We are to be of the same mind toward one another (see Rom. 12:16; 15:5).
We are to edify one another (see Rom. 14:19).
We are to accept one another (see Rom. 15:7).
We are to instruct one another (see Rom. 15:14).
We are to greet one another (see Rom. 16:16; 1 Cor. 16:20; 2 Cor. 13:12; 1 Thess. 5:26; 1 Pet. 5:14).
We are to bear with one another (see Eph. 4:2; Col. 3:13).
We are to be kind to one another (see Eph. 4:32).
We are to submit to one another (see Eph. 5:21; 1 Pet. 5:5).
We are to esteem one another (see Phil. 2:3).
We are to offer hospitality to one another (see 1 Pet. 4:9).
We are to fellowship with one another (see 1 John 1:7).

Without question, when members of the local church faithfully practice these one-another injunctions, the Body of Christ will "build itself up in love" (Eph. 4:16). We will experience what the apostle Paul identified as "the greatest of these."

Guiding Principles

Principle 1. When measuring a church, we must evaluate the degree to which a local community of believers is reflecting true love and unity.

In order to effectively apply this principle, we must begin by looking at the spiritual leaders in any given church, especially those who are responsible to "be shepherds of God's flock" (1 Pet. 5:2). Are these overseers loving one another as Christ loved them and functioning as a godly, unified *ekklesia* (assembly), "being examples to the flock" (1 Pet. 5:3)?

Jesus Christ modeled this principle for us when He washed the disciples' feet. How could these men plant churches that would become loving and unified communities of faith when they had not been serving one another in love (see Gal. 5:13)?

Jesus, of course, worked with what He had when He chose these men. When He first called them to follow Him, they were certainly not qualified to carry out the Great Commission. Jesus spent nearly three years getting them ready for this great task and did not entrust them with this responsibility until they were prepared.

Just so, we must not hand over the highest level of leadership in a church to individuals who are not qualified. This is why we must take very seriously the requirements for spiritual leaders outlined by Paul in his letters to Timothy and Titus (see 1 Tim. 3:1-13; Titus 1:5-9). This is also why I have devoted the next chapter, titled "Measuring Our Leaders," to looking carefully at these qualities. The fact is that it only takes one or two powerful, carnal leaders in a church to literally destroy that ministry. This is why these requirements are so important; biblically qualified leaders will reflect the unity Christ prayed for. It is this dynamic that also impacts the Church.

Principle 2. When measuring a church, we must evaluate the degree to which all members of that local community are committed to obeying Christ's command to "love one another."

Jesus Christ gave the apostles a new commandment, to "love one another" (John 13:34; 15:17). He then informed them that if they really loved Him, they would obey this new commandment (see John 15:9-10).

Once their hearts and minds were enlightened by the Holy Spirit, the apostles did what Jesus challenged them to do. Furthermore, they taught others—namely, all of us who have received the Lord Jesus Christ as personal Savior—to do the same.

As we've seen, the authors of the New Testament letters—primarily the apostles—again and again instruct all of us as believers to practice Jesus' new commandment to "love one another." In evaluating any church, we must discover the extent to which people are obeying this new commandment. This will be the true test of our love for God and our love for our brothers and sisters in Christ.

One day when Jesus was asked which was the greatest commandment in the law of Moses, He elaborated on His new commandment, adding both the vertical and horizontal dimensions:

> "Love the Lord your God with all your heart and with all your soul and with all your mind." This is the first and greatest commandment. And the second is like it: "Love your neighbor as yourself." All the Law and the Prophets hang on these two commandments (Matt. 22:37-40).

Principle 3. When measuring a church, we must evaluate the degree to which all believers are participating in building up the Body of Christ in love by faithfully practicing the "one-another" injunctions.

Unfortunately, some churches put the cart in front of the horse. They focus on giftedness rather than on biblical functions, not realizing that this can lead to a spiritually unhealthy introspection. Furthermore, it can cause some immature believers to be lifted up with pride and to even become self-deceived—thinking they have certain gifts that they really do not have.

When this happens, it sometimes leads to judgmental attitudes, divisions and even a subtle arrogance—both within individual believers and within the church as a whole—can be the results.

As we have seen, the Bible emphasizes functions—those things all believers are to do for one another. When we measure a church, we must look for the extent to which believers are being taught these injunctions and the extent to which they are practicing them. As I shared earlier, when I began to emphasize these one-another injunctions in the churches I have planted and pastored, the Body of Christ began to build itself up in love as never before. I found that I didn't have to talk about discovering and using gifts and abilities. This happened naturally in the context of a growing maturity.

THINKING AND GROWING TOGETHER

1. Why does Satan consistently attempt to destroy love and unity in a local church? What are his specific tactics, and what happens when he achieves this insidious goal?
2. How can we defeat Satan and keep him from destroying love and unity in the church? (See Eph. 4:1-6; 6:10-18; Phil. 2:1-8.)
3. What suggestions would you give a church that would like to begin to practice more faithfully the one-another injunctions outlined on pages 189-190?

Note

1. Henry Drummond, *The Greatest Thing in the World* (New York: Grosset and Dunlap, 1900), n.p.

CHAPTER 9

MEASURING OUR LEADERS

Up to this point, we have considered how we can measure a local church—a community of believers that form an *ekklesia*. There is a segment of a church, however, that should definitely reflect "the whole measure of the fullness of Christ," both in their personal and corporate character. I am referring, of course, to the spiritual leaders in that church.[1]

At the highest level, these leaders were identified as elders or bishops in the New Testament. These terms were used interchangeably, particularly by Paul, and they described the people who served as permanent pastors. They were to manage and oversee each local body of believers. Without shepherds, sheep will go astray. In the same way, without *spiritual shepherds*, God's sheep will not grow spiritually and will never become mature believers.

This is why Paul and Barnabas returned to the Galatian cities where they had planted churches on their first missionary journey and "appointed elders . . . in each church" (Acts 14:23). This is also why Paul left Titus in Crete with instructions to "appoint elders in every town" where they had planted churches (Titus 1:5). However, as we will learn, Paul made it crystal clear to both Timothy and Titus that they were to designate elders *only* if the appointees were mature believers.

Mature Leaders Needed

Mature spiritual leaders are unquestionably the key to producing a mature church. Believers must be led by pastors who have already moved from childhood to adulthood in their spiritual lives. If the whole church is to become like Christ, reflecting faith, hope and love, its members must have godly models who are already reflecting these qualities.

How can we recognize mature leaders? Paul offered a specific answer. He wanted Timothy, Titus and each of us to discern maturity in a potential spiritual leader (see 1 Tim. 3:1-7; Titus 1:5-9). When we study these qualities carefully, we will note that very little, if anything, is said about skills, abilities or even spiritual gifts. Each of the characteristics Paul lists relate to qualities of life: high moral and ethical behavior, right attitudes, pure motives, proper goals, positive habits and quality relationships. Moreover, each quality helps build a good reputation—within and outside the church.

A careful study of Paul's letters reveals that not even knowledge is high on his list of preferred attributes for church leaders. However, he obviously assumes that a leader will have a certain amount of information and understanding; particularly in his letter to Titus when he said a leader ought to "hold firmly to the trustworthy message as it has been taught, so that he can encourage others by sound doctrine and refute those who oppose it" (Titus 1:9).

There is a good reason for placing an emphasis on character rather than emphasizing the need to choose people who have a lot of knowledge and skills. Gifted people who do not reflect the qualities outlined by Paul can subtly lead people in the wrong direction—sometimes very quickly. This was happening in Ephesus and Crete when Paul outlined the qualifications for elders in his letters to Timothy and Titus (see 1 Tim. 1:3-4; Titus 1:10-14).[2]

As noted earlier, Paul gives us two lists. However, because of space limitations, let's concentrate on the characteristics outlined in 1 Timothy and then include supplementary references to those listed in his letter to Titus.

Above Reproach (see 1 Tim. 3:2; Titus 1:6)

Paul put this quality at the top of the list in both of his letters. He, of course, was not insisting upon perfection, because Jesus Christ was the only perfect leader who ever walked—or will walk—on planet Earth. Rather, Paul was referring to *our reputation*—how others view us.

Timothy's character was perhaps his greatest strength as a leader. This was the basic reason why Paul asked him to serve as his assistant in ministry. When Paul and Silas arrived in Lystra on their second missionary journey, Luke recorded that "the brothers at Lystra and Iconium *spoke well* of him" (Acts 16:2). People were talking about this young man and his commitment to Jesus Christ, not only where he lived but also in a neighboring city. His reputation had spread beyond his local community.

Paul was impressed with Timothy's qualifications because he knew the challenge that lay ahead. If new congregations were to mature in Christ, they would need godly leaders. Even though he was a relatively young man, Timothy met Paul's expectations. In addition, if Timothy was going to be able to discover and approve local church leaders, he needed to be a young man who practiced what he preached.

Just One Wife (see 1 Tim. 3:2; Titus 1:6)

When Paul exhorted Timothy to appoint men as elders who had been "the husband of but one wife," he was referring to moral purity. We could fairly translate Paul's phrase as a "man of one woman." In other words, any man who served the church as an elder or pastor was to have sexual relations with only one woman in his life—specifically, his wife.

One reason this was such an important spiritual requirement in the New Testament world is that many men—particularly those who were rich—related at a sexual level to more than one woman. Besides a wife, a wealthy man had easy access to his favorite slave girl. Furthermore, because of his pagan religion, he often visited a prostitute down at the local temple. This was a common practice within the Roman Empire. However, when a man became a Christian, he came face-to-face with a new moral requirement: God's standard. He was to have sexual intimacy with only one woman in his life, his legal wife. The same standard, of course, applied to a Christian woman. She was to have a sexual relationship with only one man in her life—her husband.

In both letters, being the "husband of but one wife" is listed second after being "above reproach." This is definitely by divine design. Moral purity is the most important quality for building a good reputation. Any Christian leader who violates this principle becomes suspect in terms of being trustworthy. Unfortunately, we have had some tragic illustrations of this reality in the lives of some of our most recognizable pastors and evangelists as well as our highest elected officials, including the president of the United States. Adultery and lying always go hand-in-hand, unless there is absolute and total repentance.[3]

Temperate (see 1 Tim. 3:2)

When Paul used the term "temperate," he was describing leaders who have a clear focus on life. They have a biblical view of history, understanding God's sovereign control of the universe. At the same time, they carry out human responsibilities diligently. They are balanced in approaching problems, and they avoid extremes that sidetrack them from carrying out the purposes God left all of us to fulfill in the world.

In his letter to the Thessalonians, Paul described temperate Christians as those who have put "on *faith* and *love* as a breastplate, and the *hope* of salvation as a helmet" (1 Thess. 5:8). As we have seen, Paul used this divine trilogy frequently as a general measurement of maturity among Christians. If all of us together are to reflect these qualities, we need godly leaders who first and foremost model faith, hope and love. Being temperate is an important reflection of these qualities.

Prudent (see 1 Tim. 3:2)

The Greek word translated "prudent" is *sophron*, which literally means being "sound in mind." This word can also be translated "discreet," "sober," "sensible" or "self-controlled." Frankly, I like the word "prudent."

When Moses faced the awesome responsibility of leading more than 2 million people through the wilderness, he was directed by the Lord to "choose some wise, understanding and respected men" (Deut. 1:13-14) from each tribe and to appoint them as leaders to help in his own management role. In short, wise, understanding and respected people are prudent leaders.

Respectable (see 1 Tim. 3:2)

The Greek word translated "respectable" is *kosmios.* Our English word "cosmetics" comes from the same basic root. We see this connection when the verb *kosmeo* is translated "to adorn." For example, slaves were to be well pleasing and not argumentative, and they were not to steal from their masters. Instead, they were to "adorn [*kosmeo*] the doctrine of God our Savior in all things"

If all Christians are going to learn how to show hospitality—and they should—then they need to see it modeled in their leaders.

(Titus 2:10, *NKJV*). In essence, Paul was teaching that our lives as leaders should be like cosmetics to the gospel. When non-Christians observe our attitudes and actions, they should be attracted to the gospel message. Just as cosmetics attract people to us physically, respectable (*kosmios*) leaders attract people to Jesus Christ.

Hospitable (see 1 Tim. 3:2)

Generally speaking, "hospitality" describes the way we should use our material possessions—particularly the homes we live in and the food we eat. Look closely at the following biblical exhortations:

> Be devoted to one another in *brotherly love.* Honor one another above yourselves. Share with God's people who are in need. Practice hospitality (Rom. 12:10,13).

> Above all, *love each other deeply*, because love covers over a multitude of sins. *Offer hospitality* to one another without grumbling (1 Pet. 4:8-9).

If *all* Christians are going to learn how to show hospitality—and they should—then they need to see it modeled in their leaders. This was very important in the early days of Christianity because a church could not own property; consequently, believers had to meet in homes, especially in the homes of church leaders. Although cultural situations have changed, it is still very important that a Christian leader be generous—and a specific reflection of that generosity is hospitality.

Able to Teach (see 1 Tim. 3:2)

On the surface, it may appear that Paul was referring to the gift of teaching, or an ability or skill in communication. Not so—at least not in the way we think of preaching and teaching methods today. Rather, to be "able to teach" is a quality of life, an aspect of a leader's character.

The Greek word translated "able to teach" is *didaktikos*, and is used only twice in the New Testament—first in Paul's initial letter to Timothy and then in his second letter. In 2 Timothy, Paul described how this quality functions (see 2 Tim. 2:24-25). Take note of the words Paul used that cluster around the quality of being "able to teach." He exhorted Timothy to not be quarrelsome or argumentative. He was to be kind to everyone, referring specifically to everyone with whom he was having a conversation. And while communicating, he was to be patient when wronged. When anyone opposed the message of the Word of God, he was to correct with gentleness. We reflect these qualities of maturity when we are nondefensive in our communication. In fact, in classical Greek, the word *didaktikos* meant "teachable." Several hundred years later, when this word was translated from the classical Greek into *koine*—the language of the New Testament—it meant "to be able to teach with a teachable spirit." Paul says this is a definite reflection of maturity.

Not Be Addicted to Wine (see 1 Tim. 3:3)

Most scholars agree that references to wine in both the Old and New Testaments refer to fermented grape juice. This is why Paul wrote that a spiritual leader should not be "addicted to wine." Obviously though, Paul was not teaching total abstinence; otherwise, he would have stated that a spiritual leader should never partake of wine.

What does the Bible actually teach about drinking wine?

It is always outside God's will to overindulge and overdrink (see Prov. 23:29-30).

It is always outside God's will to become addicted to wine (see 1 Cor. 6:12).

It is always outside God's will when we cause others to sin (see Rom. 14:21).

It is always outside God's will to become addicted to anything—drugs, material things, food, etc. (see Prov. 23:20-21).

In our culture, many Christian leaders choose to totally abstain from alcoholic beverages so as not to cause any Christian to stumble and become addicted. This was Paul's perspective when he wrote to the Romans and said: "It is better not to eat meat or drink wine or to do anything else that will cause your brother to fall" (Rom. 14:21).

Not Pugnacious (see 1 Tim. 3:3)

In the Greek the word translated "pugnacious" is *plektees.* It can mean to strike out at someone physically or to be verbally pugnacious, contentious or quarrelsome.

Pugnaciousness is really anger out of control. It is not surprising that Paul stated this requirement for spiritual leaders following his warning against being "addicted to wine." Drinking, and particularly drunkenness, often leads to arguments, brawls and fights.

Even more fundamental than not being pugnacious is to avoid being quick-tempered. Paul referred to this characteristic in his letter to Titus (see 1:7). Quick-temperedness is also a form of anger.

At this point, we must understand that not all anger is sinful. It is a normal emotion. Paul acknowledged this when he admonished the Ephesians: "In your anger do not sin" (Eph. 4:26). Jesus Christ, the perfect Son of God, demonstrated that it is possible to express anger without sinning when He drove the money changers from the temple (see John 2:13-17).

When does anger become sinful for us?

Anger becomes sinful when it results in quick-tempered behavior. A quick-tempered person flies off the handle, loses control and usually says and does things that hurt and offend others.

Our anger becomes sinful when it causes physical harm to a person. This is what Paul had in mind when he used the Greek word *plektees.* This happens when anger gets out of control.

Anger becomes sinful when it persists and results in bitterness (see Eph. 4:26).

Anger becomes sinful when we turn vengeful. Paul wrote: "Do not repay anyone evil for evil. Do not take revenge, my friends, but leave room for God's wrath: for it is written, 'It is mine to avenge; I will repay,' says the Lord" (Rom. 12:17,19).

Gentle (see 1 Tim. 3:3)

Paul contrasts pugnaciousness with gentleness. Interestingly, several Greek words are translated "gentle." Paul, however, chose this particular word, *epieikes*, to describe a particular kind of gentleness: "a spirit of forbearance." Other words that describe this kind of gentleness include equitable, fair and reasonable.

Uncontentious (see 1 Tim. 3:3)

I have a close friend who serves with me as a lay elder. Those who have known him best call him Mister Charge Ahead. In his younger days, he was known as Fast Eddie. He loved to debate, which at times was interpreted as being argumentative, insensitive and even contentious.

Before this man was selected to be an elder, we followed a standard procedure we regularly use in evaluating whether a man and his wife are qualified. We ask all our other elders, the elders' wives, our staff pastors and staff pastors' wives to fill out an evaluation form for each prospective candidate and his wife, if he is married. This form is based on the characteristics we are studying. We ask each person to use a seven-point scale to express his or her degree of satisfaction or dissatisfaction with this person's behavior as it relates to each characteristic.[4]

When Eddie was being considered for eldership, and the forms were returned, he was consistently marked down in several related areas, one being contentiousness. As senior pastor, I and one other lay elder sat down with this man and his wife to report the survey results. Frankly, I was nervous about doing this, as I always am in these circumstances. This kind of communication is always difficult for me, especially when it involves a close friend.

A wonderful thing happened. Eddie was obviously surprised, but he sat and listened. He thanked us for our time and openness with him and assured us he would think and pray about what we had shared.

He asked his wife, who had received perfect scores, for her opinion. Did she agree with our evaluation? She did, which surprised him. In retrospect, he wrote the following personal account of what had happened:

> When Maureen said that she agreed with the evaluation that I could be contentious, argumentative and too bold in defending the views I held strongly, I knew that God wanted to get my attention—big time. I also knew down deep that the evaluation was correct. As I asked God for help, He made it clear to me that I needed to develop the fruit of the Spirit known as gentleness. He also gave me a plan. I was to get my family to hold me accountable. One evening I called my family together and asked each one to forgive me for not being gentle and to ask for their help. I explained to them that every time they saw me using my verbal skills to steamroll over them, raise my voice, show anger or be contentious in any way, they were to put an *X* on the family calendar in the kitchen.
>
> To my dismay, the next day I got five *X*s. I considered changing the rules! But I was committed and my family helped me learn to be gentle. What started out as a crushing blow to my Mister Charge Ahead ego had turned into a wonderful blessing in my life. I now know words spoken in gentleness with energy are much more acceptable and effective with the listener. I certainly have not arrived at my goal, but I'm on my way.

The changes Eddie made were immediately obvious to all of us who knew him well. Eventually, he became an elder and has served with me in the ministry for a number of years. He has a heart for God, a heart for the ministry and a heart for people. Although in some respects this had been a difficult process, it produced some very significant and permanent changes in my friend's life.

Free from the Love of Money (see 1 Tim. 3:3)

Mature Christian leaders do not love money. This is true of all mature believers. The Scriptures do not teach that money in itself is evil. Nor do they teach that it is wrong to have lots of money. What they do teach is that it is a serious violation of God's will when we love money. That is why Paul said that when a Christian is selected for a leadership position in the church, that person should be free, not from money, but "from the love of money."

If people in the Church are to be taught to be generous with their incomes, then we must have leaders who model generosity.

I had the unique experience of joining a group of men who studied everything the Bible says about material possessions. To our amazement, we discovered that God says more about the way Christians should use their material possessions than any other subject other than God Himself. Unquestionably, the greatest hallmark of Christian maturity is generosity.

Research tells us that the average Christian gives only about 2 percent of his or her income to the Lord. This simply indicates that most believers in our culture are lovers of money. Christians as a whole have become materialists, which is a direct violation of the will of God.

If people in the Church are to be taught to be generous with their incomes–which for my wife and me involves a minimum of 10 percent of our gross income–then we must have leaders who model generosity. We cannot expect people to do what we do not do ourselves.

Manage His Own Family Well (see 1 Tim. 3:4)

Paul viewed a well-ordered family as a true test of a man's maturity and ability to lead other Christians. When the whole household is committed to Christ, we can be sure the father is spiritually and psychologically mature. If a man whose household is not well ordered is appointed as a spiritual leader, then the church will experience the same problems as his family. The very weaknesses that make this man a poor husband and dad will cause him to be a poor leader in the church. Furthermore, if a man who is not a good leader at home accepts this kind of leadership role, his family members will have less respect for him, which in turn will cause greater problems.

Do not misunderstand! Paul was not saying that we have to be married and we must have children in order to be good leaders. Rather, if we *are* married, and *if* we have children, then we should *have* well-ordered households.

We must also note that Paul was not disqualifying potential leaders based on natural phases their children go through as they grow up. He does, however, warn against grown children who still live in the family complex and are guilty of "being wild" and "disobedient" (Titus 1:6). More specifically, he was referring to a lifestyle that is characterized by riotous living and immorality. The rebellious sons of Eli, who served as priests in the Tabernacle, illustrate what Paul had in mind (see 1 Sam. 2:12). Eli did not "manage his own family well," and that's a major reason why he failed so miserably as a spiritual leader in Israel.

GUIDING PRINCIPLES

Principle 1. When measuring a church, we should evaluate the degree to which spiritual leaders are biblically qualified.

The characteristics Paul outlined in 1 Timothy can be summarized and succinctly defined as follows:

- Spiritual leaders in the church should be living exemplary lives that are obvious to both Christians and non-Christians.
- Spiritual leaders should be morally pure, maintaining God's standard of righteousness.
- Spiritual leaders should be temperate, which means they walk by faith, demonstrate hope and manifest true biblical love in all of their relationships.
- Spiritual leaders should be wise, show discernment and have experience.
- Spiritual leaders should live well-ordered lives that make the Word of God attractive to believers and unbelievers.
- Spiritual leaders should be unselfish and generous, willing to open their homes for ministry and to share their material possessions.
- Spiritual leaders should be able to communicate in non-argumentative, nondefensive and nonthreatening ways—demonstrating gentleness, patience and teachability, without compromising the message of the Word of God.
- Spiritual leaders should not be in bondage to any sinful cravings of the flesh; furthermore, they should carefully consider the way their freedoms in Christ might lead others to sin.

- Spiritual leaders should be able to control angry feelings and should never express these emotions in hurtful ways or allow them to linger.
- Spiritual leaders should be able to demonstrate strong convictions and directness in taking a stand for righteousness, but they should also be able to balance these attitudes and actions with a gentle and loving spirit.
- Spiritual leaders should relate to others by communicating in a manner that does not make others feel controlled, manipulated or defensive.
- Spiritual leaders should be generous Christians, giving regularly, systematically, proportionately and joyfully to the Lord's work.
- Spiritual leaders who are parents should have good relationships with their children and give proper direction to the family unit.

Principle 2. When measuring a church, we must evaluate the degree to which all believers in that body are challenged to cultivate the same qualities in their lives that Paul outlined for leaders.

It is important to understand that the criteria for selecting leaders in the church are not just a profile for pastors, elders or deacons. Rather, what Paul outlined in his letters to Timothy and Titus are the marks of a mature Christian. In essence, Paul was stating: "If you want to be a spiritual leader in the Church, that's great! But just make sure you are mature!" He then spelled out what a mature Christian looks like, whether male or female. The specific characteristics Paul pulled together in these succinct and power-packed paragraphs are listed elsewhere in the New Testament as marks of maturity for all Christians.

Principle 3. When measuring a church, we must remember that Paul was not looking for perfection in the leadership.

The Bible does not teach that we have to be perfect to become spiritual leaders. If that were true, we would all be disqualified—along with the apostle Paul (see Phil. 3:12-14). Along the way, all of us fail in certain areas of our lives. The mark of true spiritual maturity, however, is what we do about our weaknesses. Mature Christians are open to correction and take steps to make changes.

Principle 4. When measuring a church, we must remember that the maturity level in a local church will not rise above the maturity of its leadership.

Again, this is a biblical key for producing a mature church. People are basically followers and imitators. Paul understood this principle in his own ministry. This is why he wrote to the Corinthians: "Follow my example, as I follow the example of Christ" (1 Cor. 11:1).

Becoming even more specific, he wrote to the Thessalonians, reflecting on his ministry and that of his fellow missionaries, Silas and Timothy:

> You are witnesses, and so is God, of how holy, righteous and blameless we were among you who believed. For you know that we dealt with each of you as a father deals with his own children, encouraging, comforting and urging you to live lives worthy of God, who calls you into his kingdom and glory (1 Thess. 2:10-12).

Thinking and Growing Together

1. What can happen in a church when spiritual leaders are selected and appointed who are not mature in Christ?
2. How can we make sure that spiritual leaders are appointed who measure up to the qualities outlined by Paul in 1 Timothy 3:1-12 and Titus 1:5-9?
3. Since these qualities are goals for every Christian, how would you measure your own maturity in each of the categories listed in this chapter?

Notes

1. Gene Getz, "Becoming a Spiritually Mature Leader," in *Leaders on Leadership* (Ventura, CA: Regal Books, 1997), pp. 81-108.
2. In Paul's letter to Timothy, he also outlined character qualities for people who were in other serving positions—deacons and deaconesses. These were people who worked closely with local church elders. In essence, Paul outlined the same basic qualifications for these people (see 1 Tim. 3:8-12).
3. I do not believe being a husband of "one wife" refers to divorce and remarriage. As stated in the main body of this text, Paul was referring to moral purity. This also means he was not referring to polygamy—since this practice was outlawed in the Roman Empire. The important point of application is that any spiritual leader must have a good reputation both in the Christian and non-Christian community regarding marital fidelity. For more information, see Gene A. Getz, *The Measure of a Man* (Ventura, CA: Regal Books, 1995).
4. To view this scale, see Gene. A. Getz, *Measure of a Man* (Ventura, CA: Regal Books, 1995), pp. 277-280.

CHAPTER 10

MEASURING CORPORATE WORSHIP

One of the greatest challenges we all face as spiritual leaders is how to move churches from where they are in their spiritual journey to where God wants them to be. It is one thing to know *the way* God measures our maturity—the subject of this book. However, it is quite another thing to know *how* to produce this kind of maturity in order to measure up to "the fullness of Christ" (Eph. 4:13).

As I stated in the introduction to this book, I have had the privilege of launching a number of churches over the last 30 years. This challenging experience began in the late 1970s when a small group of people had heard about the biblical studies on the church that I had been developing with my students at Dallas Theological Seminary. Consequently, they invited me to share my conclusions one evening in one of their homes.

That night all of us—about 20 people in all—developed a keen sense of excitement about launching a new church. Though these people did not initially ask me to change my vocation from professor to pastor, they made it very clear that they wanted my wife and me to take primary leadership in this new venture. We agreed to the request and began to meet as a small group to raise and answer some very basic questions.

First, what kind of worship experiences do believers need in order to become a church that measures up to God's standard, reflecting faith, hope and love? We were in agreement, of course, that all of these experiences must grow out of the activities and functions outlined and described in the New Testament.

Second, once we outlined what we believed these biblical experiences were, we then discussed what kind of forms and structures we needed to develop in order to provide all of us with these experiences. Since we were launching a new church, one of our first decisions was that we would not do things in a certain way just because others had done them that way before. However, we also decided we would not be different just to be different. Rather, we wanted to develop patterns and use methods in our own cultural moment that would help us do the very best possible job we could in providing believers with biblical experiences.

Third, we wanted to be totally open to the divine leading of the Holy Spirit. After all, Jesus said that He would build His Church (see Matt. 16:18). Furthermore, Jesus said that He would answer if we would ask for His help (see Luke 11:9). As a result, prayer, both personal and corporate, became a vital part of our planning.

At this point, Luke's description of the worship activities and functions of the church in Jerusalem became for all of us a very basic and foundational passage of Scripture (Acts 2:42-47). We already knew that these experiences were frequently repeated throughout the rest of the New Testament. However, Luke brought them all together in one succinct and descriptive paragraph in which he outlined them in a very important sequence.

THE FOUNDATION OF TRUE WORSHIP

The Apostles' Teaching

In describing this new and growing church in Jerusalem, Luke began by informing us that these new believers "devoted themselves to the *apostles' teaching*" (Acts 2:42). Not only was this experience a *part* of their worship, it was also the *foundation* for their worship.

This raises some very important questions. What was the apostles' teaching? Where did it come from? And why is this experience so foundational for all of us to experience true worship?

Direct Revelation

What Peter and the other apostles taught from that day forward was what they had learned from Jesus Christ Himself. Furthermore, they were able to teach additional truths because of the messages they received from the Holy Spirit. This unusual process was a direct fulfillment of what Jesus had promised the apostles when He was with them during and following the Passover meal:

> All this I have spoken while still with you. But the Counselor, the Holy Spirit, whom the Father will send in my name, will teach you all things and will remind you of everything I have said to you (John 14:25-26).

Jesus promised the apostles two things. First, the Holy Spirit would actually reiterate those things that Jesus Christ had taught them during the relatively brief time they traveled with Him. It is clear from the Gospel records that Jesus had communicated many things to the apostles they had forgotten or had never understood. But once He died and rose again, Jesus "opened their minds so they could understand the Scriptures" (Luke 24:45). At that point, they began to really comprehend why Jesus Christ had come in the first place.

Second, there were many things that Jesus had *not* taught them while He was with them. Jesus promised that the Spirit of truth (see John 14:17; 15:26; 16:13) would *continue the process of teaching*:

> I have much more to say to you, more than you can now bear. But when he, the Spirit of truth, comes, he will guide you into all truth (John 16:12-13).

On the Day of Pentecost, the Lord's promises began to be fulfilled in the lives of the apostles. The Holy Spirit's teaching ministry initially enabled these men to proclaim the gospel. But God's Spirit also began to unfold a body of truth so that they could teach believers how to live their new lives in Christ.

The Inspired Scriptures

I believe that the Holy Spirit endowed the apostles with a special gift of teaching that enabled them to eventually author the many reports and letters included in the New Testament. Through this process, God made it possible for all of us, including those of us living in the twenty-first century, to devote ourselves to the apostles' teaching. Although we cannot hear Peter preach as he did on the Day of Pentecost, we can read the letters he wrote by the inspiration of the Holy Spirit. We cannot listen to the apostle John teach as he stood by Peter's side in those early days. However, we can read the Gospel he wrote, as well as his three epistles and that wonderful culminating document, the book of Revelation.

Paul, of course, was not converted until after Pentecost. However, he was later called to be an apostle, and the Holy Spirit enabled him to author more letters than any other New Testament writer.

In essence, the New Testament Scriptures contain those very doctrines that believers in Jerusalem were being taught in those early days of the Church. However, for us, these teaching have been beautifully and realistically woven into a variety of written documents, many of which were penned directly to New Testament churches to help them become mature.

The Word of God is foundational to true worship. Without it we would not know about faith, hope and love. Without the Scriptures, we would not know what Paul stated about real worship in Romans:

> Therefore, I urge you, brothers, in view of God's mercy, to offer your bodies as living sacrifices, holy and pleasing to God–*this is your spiritual act of worship* (Rom. 12:1).

The Essence of True Worship

Fellowship

A statement by the leader of the notorious seven who escaped from a Texas prison had a deep impact on me. When captured, George Rivas, who had confessed to fatally shooting a police officer, stated *why* he chose the six other men to plan and orchestrate their escape. "There is security in numbers," he said. "And we knew each other. Whatever weaknesses one of us had, the more people that stuck together, the more strength we had."[1]

This demonstrates a great biblical truth. Although a person may not know the Lord Jesus Christ as Savior, and even though that person may violate the laws of God in hideous ways, he or she still needs other people. We were created for *community* and not even sin can obliterate that need.

When God decided to create mankind, He said, "Let *us* make man in our image, in *our* likeness" (Genesis 1:26). With this statement, God identified Himself as the divine community: Father, Son and Holy Spirit. And when He created us, we were made in His image. We were designed for community, not to function in isolation—regardless of our fallenness.

Sin, of course, has impacted our abilities to live with one another as God intended. Failure to do His will impacted the first marriage (see Gen. 3:16), and the effects of sin quickly spread to the entire family structure, resulting in the first murder. From that point forward, mankind continued to reflect God's image but in distorted ways, which led to the terrible reflections of sinful flesh so graphically described by Paul in Galatians:

> Sexual immorality, impurity and debauchery; idolatry and witchcraft; hatred, discord, jealousy, fits of rage, selfish ambition, dissensions, factions and envy; drunkenness, orgies, and the like (Gal. 5:19-21).

Thankfully, Jesus Christ came to restore what was lost in the Garden of Eden, to enable us to once again be a community of love and unity in which believers reflect the fruit of the Holy Spirit in all of our relationships. That fruit is "love, joy, peace, patience, kindness, goodness, faithfulness, gentleness and self-control" (Gal. 5:22-23).

We see this beautifully described in the Jerusalem church. These new believers "devoted themselves to the apostles' teaching," the foundation of true worship, which enabled them to experience true *koinonia* (fellowship) with God and one another, which is the *essence of true worship*.

The apostle John captured both the human and divine dimensions of this fellowship when he wrote:

> We proclaim to you what we have seen and heard, so that you also may have *fellowship* with us. And our *fellowship* is with the Father and with his Son, Jesus Christ (1 John 1:3).

It is only as believers experience this kind of true worship that they will become mature, reflecting the "fullness of Christ" (see Eph. 4:13). Stanley Grenz states it this way:

> We who are united to Christ share in the divine image that he bears. Or perhaps better stated, as we are being made like Christ, we are being transformed into the image of God. Therefore, being created in the divine image is a process which begins with conversion and continues until the great future day when God brings us into full conformity with the divine goal for us. Then we will truly be the image of God as revealed by Christ.[2]

The Elements of True Worship

Earlier I mentioned the importance of sequence in Luke's historical record. First, Luke mentioned the *foundation* of true worship, the Word of God. Second, he referred to the *essence* of true worship, fellowship with God and one another. But he then outlined four *elements* that are absolutely necessary for believers to experience this kind of divine and human fellowship.

They Ate Together

Luke recorded:

> They devoted themselves to the apostles' teaching and to the fellowship, to *the breaking of bread* (Acts 2:42).

"The breaking of bread" was a vital aspect of New Testament worship; and it involved more than having communion periodically, using token elements, such as a morsel of bread and a sip of juice. Rather, first-century believers actually participated in one another's lives by having a meal together. On occasions, these meals are identified as love feasts (see 2 Pet. 2:13; Jude 12). As we have seen, Paul severely admonished the Corinthians for misusing and abusing this meal (see 1 Cor. 11:17-34). Rather than serving as a means for true worship, it became a very selfish and carnal activity. Rather than reflecting the "fruit of the Spirit" in their relationships as they ate together, they were reflecting "the acts of the sinful nature." That is one reason why Paul identified this church as worldly and carnal.

These love feasts in the New Testament were patterned after the Passover meal, the final supper Jesus shared with His disciples before He faced the cross. During that meal, using the same elements they had been eating and drinking together in order to meet their physical needs, Jesus broke bread and passed the cup, admonishing the apostles to thereafter remember His broken body and shed blood using these elements. In the early days in the church in Jerusalem, believers went from house to house; and it appears that every time they had a meal together, they remembered the Lord's death in a special way. The once-a-year Jewish Passover meal became a regular, simple communal meal.

The important factor, however, is not how often we remember the Lord in this way, or what specific elements we use. Rather, the essence of true worship involves this kind of fellowship: eating and drinking together and at the same time remembering the death of the Lord Jesus Christ. Here we see a remarkable blend of human relationships and our relationship with God. As these first-century believers ate together (at the horizontal, human level), they also remembered the Lord together (at the vertical, divine level). They were simultaneously having fellowship with one another and fellowship with God.

They Prayed Together

In addition to devoting themselves "to the breaking of bread," they also devoted themselves "to prayer" (Acts 2:42).

True worship has always involved prayer. This was a dynamic part of this *koinonia.* As these believers prayed, they were participating in each other's lives. They not only asked God to reveal His power and presence but also to meet their human needs. This is what was taking place in Jerusalem when "they devoted

---

True worship has always involved prayer. This was a dynamic part of this koinonia. *As these believers prayed, they were participating in each other's lives.*

---

themselves to the apostles' teaching and to the fellowship, to the breaking of bread and *to prayer*" (Acts 2:42). Prayer was an essential element in their worship.

They Shared Their Material Possessions

In Jerusalem, "all the believers were together and *had everything in common*" (Acts 2:44).

To comprehend what was actually happening, we need to understand the unique cultural implications of Jewish customs.

Every year, God-fearing Jews from all over the Roman Empire made a trek to Jerusalem to worship God. It was a 50-day celebration, often involving whole families, that culminated with the Day of Pentecost.

It was on this final day that the Holy Spirit descended in Jerusalem and anointed and empowered the apostles, just as Jesus had promised (see Acts 1:8). "A violent wind came from heaven" and "tongues of fire" descended on the apostles, enabling them to share the gospel message in a variety of languages (Acts 2:1-11). As Peter stood up to explain from Scripture what was happening, thousands of Jews responded in faith, including both the Jews who lived in the vicinity of Jerusalem as well as those "God-fearing" men and women who had come from all over the Roman world, those who were identified as "Grecian Jews" (Acts 2:5). Understandably, people from other parts of the world decided to stay on in Jerusalem to see what would happen next.

This presented some unusual problems for the apostles. How could they care for the material needs of all these people? To overcome the problem, the believers who lived in Jerusalem and in the surrounding areas shared their material possessions with their brothers and sisters in Christ.

Although the cultural dynamics changed once these Christians understood that it was not God's plan to stay in Jerusalem indefinitely, many maintained their unselfish and generous spirit, a very important element in true worship. Once believers understood how gracious God had been toward them in giving the gift of His Son, how could they do less than to worship Him by being generous with their material possessions?

Like the other worship elements, this generosity was both a human and divine experience. It was human in that these believers were caring for each other's physical needs. It was divine in that anything that was given to meet the needs of others was a gift to Jesus Christ. As the Savior once said:

> And if anyone gives even a cup of cold water to one of these little ones because he is my disciple, I tell you the truth, he will certainly not lose his reward (Matt.10:42).

They Praised God Together

As these believers in Jerusalem participated in these worship experiences—eating together, praying for one another and sharing their material possessions—they were also "*praising God*" (Acts 2:47). All of these activities are interrelated elements of true worship.

Singing certainly played an integral role in this praise. Jesus modeled this experience when He concluded the Passover meal with His disciples. Mark recorded that "when they had sung a hymn, they went out to the Mount of Olives" (Mark 14:26).

The apostle Paul echoed the importance of this experience in his letters to the Colossians and the Ephesians:

> Let the word of Christ [the foundation of true worship] dwell in you richly as you teach and admonish one another with all wisdom, and as you sing psalms, hymns and spiritual songs with gratitude in your hearts to God (Col. 3:16; see also Eph. 5:18-20).

Note once again that this element of worship, praising God, was also interrelated with human relationships. As early Christians used the medium of music to teach the Word of God to each other, they also lifted their voices and hearts in praise and thanksgiving to God.

The Results of True Worship

Luke's culminating statement demonstrates the impact of true worship on unconverted people in the community. They were "*enjoying the favor of all the people.* And the Lord added to their number daily those who were *being saved*" (Acts 2:47).

This is why the Jerusalem model is such a powerful example. As the unsaved people in Jerusalem saw the *essence* of true worship reflected in these believers' love for God and one another, many responded to the apostles' teaching. They, too, wanted to have the same experiences. In actuality, they were responding to the unity and oneness they saw in this church. What Jesus had shared with the apostles, the importance of "loving one another" (John 13:34-35), was being verified in the lives of these New

---

Unsaved Jews saw that the disciples were different from those who followed other teachers. When unbelievers saw this love and unity, they were convinced that Jesus Christ had actually come from God.

Testament believers. Unsaved Jews saw that the disciples of the Lord Jesus Christ were different from those who followed other teachers and leaders. When unbelievers saw this love and unity, they were convinced that Jesus Christ had actually come from God. This, of course, was the very thing Jesus Christ had prayed for (see John 17:20-23).

This is the miracle of love and unity. When a local body of believers engages in true worship, loving each other as Christ loved them, God in Christ is fleshed out in their lives. When this happens we demonstrate to those around us that Jesus Christ was indeed God in the flesh and that He died for the sins of the world (see 1 John 3:16). The invisible God becomes visible (see 1 John 4:12). The very unity Jesus Christ has with the Father can be seen and experienced. And this is what was happening in Jerusalem. When people saw and experienced believers engaging in true worship, they responded to the message of the gospel. This is why people were added to the Church daily as they put their faith in Jesus Christ.

Guiding Principles

Principle 1. When measuring a church, we must look at the degree to which believers are devoting themselves to learning and applying the Word of God in their lives.

This is the foundation for true worship and spiritual growth. As Paul wrote to Timothy:

> All Scripture is God-breathed and is useful for teaching, rebuking, correcting and training in righteousness, so that the man of God may be thoroughly equipped for every good work (2 Tim. 3:16-17).

Unfortunately, many churches today have departed from a strong emphasis on Bible teaching. When this happens, the foundation of true worship is weakened, which in turn affects the spiritual growth in the church.

Principle 2. When measuring a church, we must look at the degree to which believers are regularly experiencing fellowship with God and one another.

This is the essence of true worship. To measure this experience, we must look for the degree to which a church does the following:

- eats together and remembers the Lord with Holy Communion;
- prays for one another as they fellowship with God;
- shares their material possessions to meet each other's needs, while utilizing this as an opportunity to worship the One who gave His life for all mankind;
- teaches one another with psalms, hymns and spiritual songs as they lift their voices in praise and thanksgiving to God.

Principle 3. When measuring a church, we must look at the degree to which that church is impacting the world and seeing people put their faith in the Lord Jesus Christ for salvation.

This is the result of true worship. A dynamic worshiping church forms a powerful bridge to those who do not know Christ.

Unfortunately, Satan is very much aware of the power of real worship, as it reflects true love and unity. Consequently, he has a two-pronged attack. On the one hand, to simulate love and unity, he attempts to get people to join religious groups that deny the true Deity of Christ. On the other hand, he attempts to destroy true love and unity in the churches that truly believe that Jesus Christ is God. When Satan succeeds, he often drives people from the true Church into a false religious system.

Thankfully, this need not happen. Satan does not have to be victorious. Christ prayed for us! Furthermore, the Word of God outlines for us what we must do to "make every effort to keep the unity of the Spirit through the bond of peace" (Eph. 4:3). We *can* defeat Satan as a body of believers when we follow Paul's instructions to the Ephesians:

> Finally, be strong in the Lord and in his mighty power. Put on the full armor of God so that you can take your stand against the devil's schemes (Eph. 6:10-11).[3]

Principle 4. When measuring a church, we must look at the degree to which these three vital experiences are balanced—learning the Word of God, fellowshipping with God and one another and witnessing to the unsaved world.

Since the New Testament allows and encourages freedom in form, some churches choose to focus on the foundation of true worship, known as the apostles' teaching (see figure 10.1). The strength in these churches relates to their theological stability. Their weaknesses lie in their emphasis on head knowledge that frequently is not translated into dynamic fellowship experiences with God and one another. Furthermore, these churches often neglect outreach and evangelism and consequently become ingrown. There is no fresh flow of new life coming into the church, a very important factor in maintaining spiritual vitality.

On the other hand, some churches emphasize fellowship, the relational and experiential dimensions of worship (see figure 10.2). Their strength is in their warm, accepting environment and the enthusiastic participation of the members. There is usually a strong sense of community. Their weakness, however, lies in their doctrinal and emotional instability. Since they are often experience oriented, rather than biblically based, they often allow feelings rather than biblical truth to impact their lives.

There is a third category of churches that emphasize reaching people for Christ (see figure 10.3). Their main strength lies in their passion to reach people with the gospel. However, their main approach is evangelistic preaching as the church gathers. Unfortunately, believers are not edified and built up through real worship. They are often starved for the deeper truths of Scripture. The consequence is a church with a lot of activity but very little depth.

God's plan, of course, is for every local church to develop forms and structures that provide believers with a balance of all three of these experiences (see figure 10.4). In order to

THINKING AND GROWING TOGETHER

1. Why is the sequence of Luke's historical record in Acts 2:42-47 so important?
2. Describe your worship experiences as a Christian. Can you identify with the believers in Jerusalem? Why or why not?
3. How can we help a church evaluate whether or not its leadership is balancing the three vital experiences?
4. Why do churches fixate on form and structure? Why are they difficult to change?
5. How can we help believers in any given culture differentiate between those things that should *never* change (biblical function) and those things that *should* change (forms and structures) in order to provide believers with true worship experiences?

Notes

1. *Dallas Morning News*, January 25, 2001, p. 10A.
2. Stanley J. Grenz, *Created for Community* (Grand Rapids, MA: Baker Books, 1998), p. 78.
3. It is important to note that as Paul enumerates the "full armor of God," each directive is in the second person plural in the Greek text. In other words, Paul was writing to exhort *each church as a community* to "take the helmet of salvation," to "stand firm, then, with the belt of truth," to "take up the shield of faith," etc.

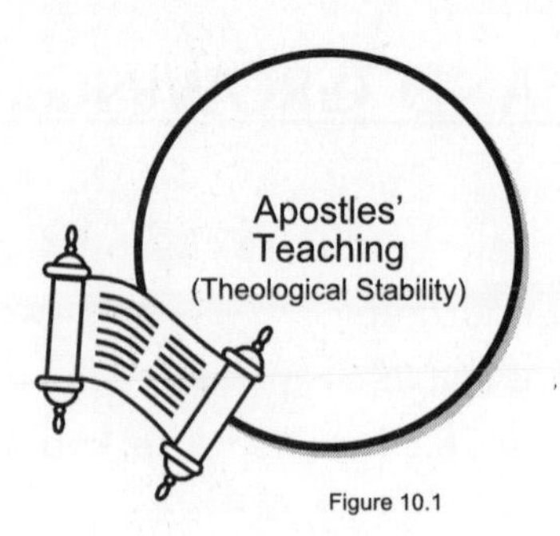

Figure 10.1

Figure 10.2

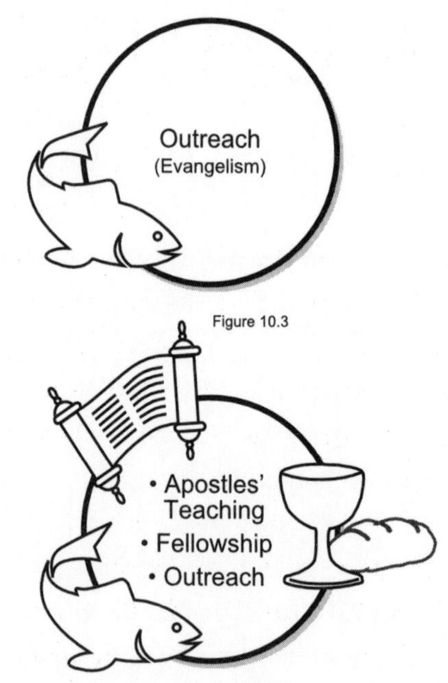

Figure 10.3

Figure 10.4

CHAPTER 11

THE MEASURE OF A CHURCH

This final chapter is designed to help you apply all of the biblical principles we have looked at in this study. These principles are summarized by chapter and each principle is followed by a question and a five-point evaluation scale.

To get the most out of this process, I suggest that you complete this exercise with a small group of dedicated Christians in your church who are sincerely committed to "attaining to the whole measure of the fullness of Christ" (Eph. 4:13)—in their own lives as well as in the life of the whole church.

It is important that you approach this assignment with humility and a prayerful attitude. Be as honest as possible, but realize that all of us tend to be somewhat subjective when it comes to evaluations. This is why it is helpful to have input from more than one person. In essence, this approach will help you to experience the Body of Christ at work.

One final suggestion: Before you complete this assignment with a group of people, read together and meditate on Paul's words to the Ephesians:

> From him [Christ] the whole body, joined and held together by every supporting ligament, grows and builds itself up in love, as each part does its work (Eph. 4:16).

Chapter 1—God's Mystery Revealed

Principle 1. When measuring a church, we can only evaluate a local, visible body of believers.

Question: To what extent do the people in our church realize how important they are as a functioning *group*—not just as functioning *individuals*?

	Little		Much	
1	2	3	4	5

Principle 2. When measuring a church, we must measure functions, not forms or structures.

Question: To what extent do the people in our church understand the difference between biblical functions and cultural forms—that functions are absolute and normative and forms are non-absolutes and should change periodically in order to carry out biblical functions at different times and in different locations?

	Little		Much	
1	2	3	4	5

Principle 3. When measuring a church, we must have a comprehensive understanding of biblical discipleship.

Question: To what extent do the people in our church understand that true disciples of Jesus are committed to obeying everything He has taught us?

Little Much

1 2 3 4 5

Principle 4. When measuring a church, we must evaluate the degree to which the true disciples in that church are functioning as a family.

Question: To what extent do the people in our church function as loving and caring brothers and sisters in Jesus Christ?

Little Much

1 2 3 4 5

Principle 5. When measuring a church, we must evaluate the degree to which believers are reflecting the fruit of the Spirit in their relationships with one another.

Question: To what extent are people in our church reflecting the fruit of the Spirit in their relationships with one another—"love, joy, peace, patience, kindness, goodness, faithfulness, gentleness and self-control" (Gal. 5:22-23)?

Little Much

1 2 3 4 5

Chapter 2—Metaphors That Measure

Principle 1. When measuring a church, we must look to the Scriptures as our final authority in faith and practice.
Question: To what extent do the people in our church believe that the Bible in its entirety is the revealed Word of God?

	Little		Much	
1	2	3	4	5

Principle 2. When measuring a church, we must have a clear understanding of the centrality of the *ekklesia* in God's scheme.
Question: To what extent are the people in our church committed first and foremost to supporting this local ministry with their time, talents and treasures?

	Little		Much	
1	2	3	4	5

Principle 3. When measuring a church, we must make sure that we have not allowed value shifts in our culture to cause us to reinterpret scriptural criteria in order to accommodate nonbiblical trends.
Question: To what extent are the people in our church being transformed into the image of Christ rather than being conformed to the world's system?

	Little		Much	
1	2	3	4	5

CHAPTER 3—THE PERFECT MEASUREMENT

Principle 1. When measuring a church, we must look for the degree to which believers have a true understanding of who the Lord Jesus Christ really is.

Question: To what extent do the people in our church understand and believe in the deity of Jesus Christ–that He and the Father are One?

	Little		Much	
1	2	3	4	5

Principle 2. When measuring a church, we must evaluate the degree to which believers reflect the life and glory of the Lord Jesus Christ.

Question: To what extent do the people in our church measure up to the fullness of Christ as a community, reflecting His character?

	Little		Much	
1	2	3	4	5

Chapter 4—Reflecting God's Grace

Principle 1. When measuring a church, we must determine the degree to which God's people understand that salvation is a free gift that results from God's grace—a gift that cannot be earned and that is eternal.

Question: To what extent do the people in our church understand and believe that salvation is an absolutely free gift and cannot be earned by good works?

	Little		Much	
1	2	3	4	5

Principle 2. When measuring a church, we must determine the degree to which God's people are motivated to live righteous and holy lives because they clearly understand and deeply appreciate God's grace in saving them.

Question: To what extent are the people in our church motivated to present their bodies to Jesus Christ as a living sacrifice because of God's great mercy in saving them?

	Little		Much	
1	2	3	4	5

Principle 3. When measuring a church, we must determine the degree to which God's people have a correct view of God's holiness.

Question: To what extent are the people in our church committed to being holy as God is holy?

	Little		Much	
1	2	3	4	5

Principle 4. When measuring a church, we must determine the degree to which God's people understand God's loving discipline.

Question: To what extent do the people in our church understand that God will discipline His children at some point in time if they persist in living outside the will of God?

	Little		Much	
1	2	3	4	5

Principle 5. When measuring a church, we must determine the degree to which God's people are extending grace to one another.

Question: To what extent do the people in our church avoid judgmental attitudes and accept one another just as Christ has accepted them?

	Little		Much	
1	2	3	4	5

Principle 6. When measuring a church, we must determine the degree to which God's people are drawing on God's grace to carry out His divine directives.

Question: To what extent do the people in our church pray for one another–and themselves–when facing difficult circumstances?

	Little		Much	
1	2	3	4	5

Chapter 5—A Divine Trilogy

Principle 1. When measuring a church, we must not evaluate spirituality on the basis of a manifestation of spiritual gifts.
Question: To what extent are the people in our church focusing on their gifts rather than on becoming like Jesus Christ in all they do?

	Little		Much	
1	2	3	4	5

Principle 2. When measuring a church, we must look for the degree to which believers are manifesting faith, hope and love—but especially love.
Question: To what extent are the people in our church manifesting faith, hope and love—but especially love?

	Little		Much	
1	2	3	4	5

CHAPTER 6—FAITH THAT WORKS

Principle 1. When measuring a church, we must determine the degree to which doctrinal stability exists in that body.
Question: To what extent do the people in our church understand and believe the basic doctrines of Christianity?

	Little		Much	
1	2	3	4	5

Principle 2. When measuring a church, we must determine the degree to which Christians in that body demonstrate that they are God's workmanship, created in Christ Jesus to do good works.
Question: To what extent are the people in our church committed to doing good works *because* of their salvation?

	Little		Much	
1	2	3	4	5

Principle 3. When measuring a church, we must determine the degree to which Christians are praying that Christ's life will be developed within them.
Question: To what extent are the people in our church praying that they will reflect the love and holiness of God Himself?

	Little		Much	
1	2	3	4	5

Chapter 7—Hope That Endures

Principle 1. When measuring a church, we must look for a full understanding of hope that is based on belief in a literal resurrection of Jesus Christ.

Question: To what extent do the people in our church believe in the literal resurrection of Jesus Christ from the dead?

	Little		Much	
1	2	3	4	5

Principle 2. When measuring a church, we must look for a full understanding of hope that assures all true believers in the Lord Jesus Christ that they have eternal life, regardless of their ethnic or religious backgrounds.

Question: To what extent do the people in our church function as one body with one hope–regardless of their ethnic, religious and economic backgrounds?

	Little		Much	
1	2	3	4	5

Principle 3. When measuring a church, we must look for a true and full understanding of hope that reflects steadfastness and endurance no matter what life's circumstances.

Question: To what extent do the people in our church reflect a sense of security and stability regardless of the changing world around them?

	Little		Much	
1	2	3	4	5

CHAPTER 8—LOVE: THE GREATEST OF THESE

Principle 1. When measuring a church, we must evaluate the degree to which a local community of believers is reflecting true love and unity.

Question: To what extent are the people in our church reflecting the love of Jesus Christ and the unity that exists in the eternal community—Father, Son and Holy Spirit?

	Little		Much	
1	2	3	4	5

Principle 2. When measuring a church, we must evaluate the degree to which all members of that local community are committed to obeying Christ's command to "love one another" (John 13:34).

Question: To what extent are the people in our church loving one another as Christ has loved them?

	Little		Much	
1	2	3	4	5

Principle 3. When measuring a church, we must evaluate the degree to which all believers are participating in building up the body of Christ in love by faithfully practicing the "one-another" injunctions.

Question: To what extent are the people in our church ministering to one another by practicing all of the "one-another" injunctions?

	Little		Much	
1	2	3	4	5

Chapter 9—Measuring Our Leaders

Principle 1. When measuring a church, we should evaluate the degree to which spiritual leaders are biblically qualified.
Question: To what extent do our spiritual leaders measure up to the qualifications outlined in 1 Timothy 3 and Titus 1?

	Little		Much	
1	2	3	4	5

Principle 2. When measuring a church, we must evaluate the degree to which all believers in that body are challenged to cultivate the same qualities in their lives that Paul outlined for leaders.
Question: To what extent are all members of our church committed to developing the same qualities in their lives that are outlined for spiritual leaders?

	Little		Much	
1	2	3	4	5

Principle 3. When measuring a church, we must remember that Paul was not looking for perfection in the leadership.
Question: To what extent do the people in our church have a realistic view of maturity—a view that does not promote perfectionism and attitudes that are self-defeating?

	Little		Much	
1	2	3	4	5

Principle 4. When measuring a church, we must remember that the maturity level in a local church will not rise above the maturity level of its leadership.

Question: To what extent are the spiritual leaders in our church serving as examples to the flock in terms of spiritual maturity?

	Little		Much	
1	2	3	4	5

Chapter 10—Measuring Corporate Worship

Principle 1. When measuring a church, we must look at the degree to which believers are devoting themselves to learning and applying the Word of God in their lives.
Question: To what extent are the people in our church being exposed to the total message of the Bible?

	Little		Much	
1	2	3	4	5

Principle 2. When measuring a church, we must look at the degree to which believers are regularly experiencing fellowship with God and one another.
Question: To what extent are the people in our church experiencing true fellowship with God and with one another in an integrated way?

	Little		Much	
1	2	3	4	5

Principle 3. When measuring a church, we must look at the degree to which that church is impacting the world and seeing people put their faith in the Lord Jesus Christ for salvation.
Question: To what extent are the people in our church reflecting love and unity to the world around them?

	Little		Much	
1	2	3	4	5

Principle 4. When measuring a church, we must look at the degree to which these three vital experiences are balanced—learning the Word of God, fellowshipping with God and one another and witnessing to the unsaved world.
Question: To what extent are the people in our church experiencing the three vital experiences?

	Little		Much	
1	2	3	4	5

Principle 5. When measuring a church, we must look at the degree to which that church allows freedom in form in providing believers with all three of these experiences, which provide true and balanced worship.
Question: To what extent are the leaders in our church free to develop new and creative forms and structures in order to carry out the unchanging biblical functions and principles outlined in the Scriptures?

	Little		Much	
1	2	3	4	5

Appendix A

Use of the Word "Church" (*Ekklesia*) in the Book of Acts and the Epistles

Bible Reference	The Universal CHURCH	A Group of Local Churches	A Specific Local Church
Acts 5:11			Church
Acts 8:1			Church
Acts 9:31		Churches	
Acts 11:22			Church
Acts 11:26			Church
Acts 12:1			Church
Acts 12:5			Church
Acts 13:1			Church
Acts 14:23			Church
Acts 14:27			Church
Acts 15:3			Church
Acts 15:4			Church
Acts 15:22			Church
Acts 15:41		Churches	
Acts 16:5		Churches	
Acts 18:22			Church
Acts 20:17			Church
Acts 20:28			Church
James 5:14			Church
Galatians 1:2		Churches	

Bible Reference	The Universal CHURCH	A Group of Local Churches	A Specific Local Church
Galatians 1:13	CHURCH		
Galatians 1:22		Churches	
1 Thessalonians 1:1			Church
1 Thessalonians 2:14		Churches	
2 Thessalonians 1:1			Church
2 Thessalonians 1:4		Churches	
1 Corinthians 1:2			Church
1 Corinthians 4:17			Church
1 Corinthians 7:17		Churches	
1 Corinthians 10:32	CHURCH		
1 Corinthians 11:16		Churches	
1 Corinthians 11:18			Church
1 Corinthians 11:22	CHURCH		
1 Corinthians 12:28	CHURCH		
1 Corinthians 14:4			Church
1 Corinthians 14:5			Church
1 Corinthians 14:12			Church
1 Corinthians 14:19			Church
1 Corinthians 14:23			Church
1 Corinthians 14:28			Church
1 Corinthians 14:33		Churches	
1 Corinthians 14:34		Churches	
1 Corinthians 14:35			Church
1 Corinthians 15:9	CHURCH		
1 Corinthians 16:1		Churches	
1 Corinthians 16:19		Churches	
2 Corinthians 1:1			Church
2 Corinthians 8:1		Churches	
2 Corinthians 8:18		Churches	
2 Corinthians 8:23		Churches	
2 Corinthians 8:24		Churches	

Bible Reference	The Universal CHURCH	A Group of Local Churches	A Specific Local Church
2 Corinthians 11:8		Churches	
2 Corinthians 11:28		Churches	
2 Corinthians 12:13		Churches	
Romans 16:1			Church
Romans 16:4		Churches	
Romans 16:5			Church
Romans 16:16		Churches	
Romans 16:23			Church
Ephesians 1:22	CHURCH		
Ephesians 3:10	CHURCH		
Ephesians 3:21	CHURCH		
Ephesians 5:23	CHURCH		
Ephesians 5:24	CHURCH		
Ephesians 5:25	CHURCH		
Ephesians 5:27	CHURCH		
Ephesians 5:29	CHURCH		
Ephesians 5:32	CHURCH		
Colossians 1:18	CHURCH		
Colossians 1:24	CHURCH		
Colossians 4:15			Church
Colossians 4:16			Church
Philippians 3:6	CHURCH		
Philippians 4:15			Church
Philemon 2			Church
1 Timothy 3:5			Church
1 Timothy 3:15	CHURCH		
1 Timothy 5:16			Church
Hebrews 2:12	CHURCH		
Hebrews 12:23	CHURCH		
3 John 6			Church
3 John 9			Church

The Universal CHURCH	**A Group of Local Churches**	**A Specific Local Church**	**Bible Reference**
3 John 10			Church
Revelation 1:4		Churches	
Revelation 1:11		Churches	
Revelation 1:20		Churches	
Revelation 1:20		Churches	
Revelation 2:1			Church
Revelation 2:7		Churches	
Revelation 2:8			Church
Revelation 2:11		Churches	
Revelation 2:12			Church
Revelation 2:17		Churches	
Revelation 2:18			Church
Revelation 2:23		Churches	
Revelation 2:29		Churches	
Revelation 3:1			Church
Revelation 3:6		Churches	
Revelation 3:7			Church
Revelation 3:13		Churches	
Revelation 3:14			Church
Revelation 3:22		Churches	
Revelation 22:16		Churches	

APPENDIX B

DESCRIPTIONS OF LOCAL CHURCH PARTICIPANTS

Bible Reference	Church(es)	Brother(s)	Saints	Believer(s)	Body	Temple	Disciple(s)	Household
Acts 1:15							X	
Acts 1:16		X						
Acts 2:44				X				
Acts 4:32				X				
Acts 5:11	X							
Acts 6:1							X	
Acts 6:2							X	
Acts 6:3		X						
Acts 8:1	X							
Acts 9:1							X	
Acts 9:10							X	
Acts 9:13			X					
Acts 9:17		X						
Acts 9:19							X	
Acts 9:25							X	
Acts 9:26a							X	
Acts 9:26b							X	
Acts 9:30		X						
Acts 9:31	X							

Bible Reference	Church(es)	Brother(s)	Saints	Believer(s)	Body	Temple	Disciple(s)	Household
Acts 9:32			X					
Acts 9:36							X	
Acts 9:38							X	
Acts 9:41			X					
Acts 10:23		X						
Acts 10:45				X				
Acts 11:1		X						
Acts 11:12		X						
Acts 11:22	X							
Acts 11:26	X							
Acts 11:29a							X	
Acts 11:29b		X						
Acts 12:1	X							
Acts 12:5	X							
Acts 12:17		X						
Acts 13:1	X							
Acts 13:52							X	
Acts 14:2		X						
Acts 14:20							X	
Acts 14:21							X	
Acts 14:22							X	
Acts 14:23	X							
Acts 14:27	X							
Acts 14:28							X	
Acts 15:1		X						
Acts 15:3a	X							
Acts 15:3b		X						
Acts 15:4	X							
Acts 15:5				X				

Bible Reference	Church(es)	Brother(s)	Saints	Believer(s)	Body	Temple	Disciple(s)	Household
Acts 15:7		X						
Acts 15:10							X	
Acts 15:13		X						
Acts 15:22a	X							
Acts 15:22b		X						
Acts 15:32		X						
Acts 15:33		X						
Acts 15:36		X						
Acts 15:40		X						
Acts 15:41	X							
Acts 16:1							X	
Acts 16:2		X						
Acts 16:5	X							
Acts 16:40		X						
Acts 17:6		X						
Acts 17:10		X						
Acts 17:14		X						
Acts 18:18		X						
Acts 18:22	X							
Acts 18:23							X	
Acts 18:27a		X						
Acts 18:27b							X	
Acts 19:1							X	
Acts 19:9							X	
Acts 19:30							X	
Acts 20:1							X	
Acts 20:7							X	
Acts 20:17	X							
Acts 20:28	X							

Bible Reference	Church(es)	Brother(s)	Saints	Believer(s)	Body	Temple	Disciple(s)	Household
Acts 20:30							X	
Acts 20:32		X						
Acts 21:4							X	
Acts 21:7		X						
Acts 21:16a							X	
Acts 21:16b							X	
Acts 21:17		X						
Acts 21:20		X						
Acts 21:25				X				
Acts 22:13		X						
Acts 26:10			X					
Acts 28:14		X						
Acts 28:15		X						
Jas. 1:2		X						
Jas. 1:9		X						
Jas. 1:16		X						
Jas. 1:19		X						
Jas. 2:1		X						
Jas. 2:5		X						
Jas. 2:14		X						
Jas. 2:15		X						
Jas. 3:1		X						
Jas. 3:10		X						
Jas. 3:12		X						
Jas. 4:11a		X						
Jas. 4:11b		X						
Jas. 5:7		X						
Jas. 5:9		X						
Jas. 5:10		X						

Bible Reference	Church(es)	Brother(s)	Saints	Believer(s)	Body	Temple	Disciple(s)	Household
Jas. 5:12		X						
Jas. 5:14	X							
Jas. 5:19		X						
Gal. 1:2a		X						
Gal. 1:2b	X							
Gal. 1:11		X						
Gal. 1:13	X							
Gal. 1:22	X							
Gal. 3:15		X						
Gal. 4:12		X						
Gal. 4:28		X						
Gal. 4:31		X						
Gal. 5:11		X						
Gal. 5:13		X						
Gal. 6:1		X						
Gal. 6:10				X				
Gal. 6:18		X						
1 Thess. 1:1	X							
1 Thess. 1:4		X						
1 Thess. 1:7				X				
1 Thess. 2:1		X						
1 Thess. 2:9		X						
1 Thess. 2:14a		X						
1 Thess. 2:14 b	X							
1 Thess. 2:17		X						
1 Thess. 3:2		X						
1 Thess. 3:7		X						
1 Thess. 3:13			X					
1 Thess. 4:1		X						

Bible Reference	Church(es)	Brother(s)	Saints	Believer(s)	Body	Temple	Disciple(s)	Household
1 Thess. 4:6		X						
1 Thess. 4:10		X						
1 Thess. 4:13		X						
1 Thess. 5:1		X						
1 Thess. 5:4		X						
1 Thess. 5:12		X						
1 Thess. 5:14		X						
1 Thess. 5:25		X						
1 Thess. 5:26		X						
1 Thess. 5:27		X						
2 Thess. 1:1	X							
2 Thess. 1:3		X						
2 Thess. 1:4	X							
2 Thess. 1:10			X					
2 Thess. 2:1		X						
2 Thess. 2:13		X						
2 Thess. 2:15		X						
2 Thess. 3:1		X						
2 Thess. 3:6 a		X						
2 Thess. 3:6 b		X						
2 Thess. 3:13		X						
2 Thess 3:15		X						
1 Cor. 1:1		X						
1 Cor. 1:2a	X							
1 Cor. 1:2b			X					
1 Cor. 1:10		X						
1 Cor. 1:11		X						
1 Cor. 1:26		X						
1 Cor. 2:1		X						

Bible Reference	Church(es)	Brother(s)	Saints	Believer(s)	Body	Temple	Disciple(s)	Household
1 Cor. 3:1		X						
1 Cor. 3:9						X		
1 Cor. 3:16						X		
1 Cor. 3:17						X		
1 Cor. 4:6		X						
1 Cor. 4:17	X							
1 Cor. 5:11		X						
1 Cor. 6:1			X					
1 Cor. 6:2			X					
1 Cor. 6:5		X						
1 Cor. 6:6		X						
1 Cor. 6:8		X						
1 Cor. 7:12		X						
1 Cor. 7:15		X						
1 Cor. 7:17	X							
1 Cor. 7:24		X						
1 Cor. 7:29		X						
1 Cor. 8:11		X						
1 Cor. 8:12		X						
1 Cor. 8:13		X						
1 Cor. 10:1		X						
1 Cor. 10:17					X			
1 Cor. 10:32	X							
1 Cor. 11:2		X						
1 Cor. 11:16	X							
1 Cor. 11:18	X							
1 Cor. 11:22	X							
1 Cor. 11:33		X						
1 Cor. 12:1		X						

Bible Reference	Church(es)	Brother(s)	Saints	Believer(s)	Body	Temple	Disciple(s)	Household
1 Cor. 12:13					X			
1 Cor. 12:27					X			
1 Cor. 12:28	X							
1 Cor. 14:4	X							
1 Cor. 14:5	X							
1 Cor. 14:6		X						
1 Cor. 14:12	X							
1 Cor. 14:19	X							
1 Cor. 14:20		X						
1 Cor. 14:22				X				
1 Cor. 14:23	X							
1 Cor. 14:26		X						
1 Cor. 14:28	X							
1 Cor. 14:33 a	X							
1 Cor. 14:33b			X					
1 Cor. 14:35	X							
1 Cor. 14:39		X						
1 Cor. 15:1		X						
1 Cor. 15:6		X						
1 Cor. 15:9	X							
1 Cor. 15:50		X						
1 Cor. 15:58		X						
1 Cor. 16:1 a	X							
1 Cor. 16:1 b			X					
1 Cor. 16:11		X						
1 Cor. 16:12a		X						
1 Cor. 16:12b		X						
1 Cor. 16:15			X					
1 Cor. 16:19	X							

Bible Reference	Church(es)	Brother(s)	Saints	Believer(s)	Body	Temple	Disciple(s)	Household
2 Cor. 1:1a		X						
2 Cor. 1:1b	X							
2 Cor. 1:1c			X					
2 Cor. 1:8		X						
2 Cor. 2:13		X						
2 Cor. 6:16						X		
2 Cor. 8:1a		X						
2 Cor. 8:1b	X							
2 Cor. 8:4			X					
2 Cor. 8:18a		X						
2 Cor. 8:18b	X							
2 Cor. 8:22		X						
2 Cor. 8:23a		X						
2 Cor. 8:23b	X							
2 Cor. 8:24	X							
2 Cor. 9:1			X					
2 Cor. 9:3		X						
2 Cor. 9:5		X						
2 Cor. 9:12			X					
2 Cor. 11:8	X							
2 Cor. 11:9		X						
2 Cor. 11:28	X							
2 Cor. 12:13	X							
2 Cor. 12:18		X						
2 Cor. 13:11		X						
2 Cor. 13:13			X					
Rom. 1:7			X					
Rom. 1:13		X						
Rom. 7:1		X						

Bible Reference	Church(es)	Brother(s)	Saints	Believer(s)	Body	Temple	Disciple(s)	Household
Rom. 7:4		X						
Rom. 8:12		X						
Rom. 8:27			X					
Rom. 8:29		X						
Rom. 10:1		X						
Rom. 11:25		X						
Rom. 12:1		X						
Rom. 12:5					X			
Rom. 12:13			X					
Rom. 14:10a		X						
Rom. 14:10b		X						
Rom. 14:15a		X						
Rom. 14:15b		X						
Rom. 14:21		X						
Rom. 15:14		X						
Rom. 15:15		X						
Rom. 15:25			X					
Rom. 15:26			X					
Rom. 15:30		X						
Rom. 15:31			X					
Rom. 16:1	X							
Rom. 16:2			X					
Rom. 16:4	X							
Rom. 16:5	X							
Rom. 16:14		X						
Rom. 16:15			X					
Rom. 16:16	X							
Rom. 16:17		X						
Rom. 16:23a	X							

Bible Reference	Church(es)	Brother(s)	Saints	Believer(s)	Body	Temple	Disciple(s)	Household
Rom. 16:23b		X						
Eph. 1:1			X					
Eph. 1:15			X					
Eph. 1:18			X					
Eph. 1:22	X							
Eph. 1:23					X			
Eph. 2:16					X			
Eph. 2:19a			X					
Eph. 2:19b								X
Eph. 2:21						X		
Eph. 3:6					X			
Eph. 3:8			X					
Eph. 3:10	X							
Eph. 3:18			X					
Eph. 3:21	X							
Eph. 4:4					X			
Eph. 4:12a					X			
Eph. 4:12b			X					
Eph. 4:16					X			
Eph. 5:3			X					
Eph. 5:23a					X			
Eph. 5:23b	X							
Eph. 5:24	X							
Eph. 5:25	X							
Eph. 5:27	X							
Eph. 5:29	X							
Eph. 5:30					X			
Eph. 5:32	X							
Eph. 6:10		X						

Bible Reference	Church(es)	Brother(s)	Saints	Believer(s)	Body	Temple	Disciple(s)	Household
Eph. 6:18			X					
Eph. 6:21		X						
Eph. 6:23		X						
Col. 1:1		X						
Col. 1:2a		X						
Col. 1:2b			X					
Col. 1:4			X					
Col. 1:12			X					
Col. 1:18a					X			
Col. 1:18b	X							
Col. 1:24a					X			
Col. 1:24b	X							
Col. 1:26			X					
Col. 2:19					X			
Col. 3:15					X			
Col. 4:7		X						
Col. 4:9		X						
Col. 4:15a	X							
Col. 4:15b		X						
Col. 4:16	X							
Phil. 1:1			X					
Phil. 1:12		X						
Phil. 1:14		X						
Phil. 2:25		X						
Phil. 3:1		X						
Phil. 3:6	X							
Phil. 3:13		X						
Phil. 3:17		X						
Phil. 4:1		X						

Bible Reference	**Church(es)**	**Brother(s)**	**Saints**	**Believer(s)**	**Body**	**Temple**	**Disciple(s)**	**Household**
Phil. 4:8		X						
Phil. 4:15	X							
Phil. 4:21a		X						
Phil. 4:21b			X					
Phil. 4:22			X					
Philem. 1		X						
Philem. 2	X							
Philem. 5			X					
Philem. 7a		X						
Philem. 7b			X					
Philem. 16		X						
Philem. 20		X						
1 Tim. 3:5	X							
1 Tim. 3:15a								X
1 Tim. 3:15b	X							
1 Tim. 4:6		X						
1 Tim. 4:12				X				
1 Tim. 5:1		X						
1 Tim. 5:10			X					
1 Tim. 5:16	X							
1 Tim. 6:2a		X						
1 Tim. 6:2b				X				
2 Tim. 4:21		X						
1 Pet. 1:22		X						
1 Pet. 2:5								X
1 Pet. 3:8		X						
1 Pet. 4:17								X
1 Pet. 5:9		X						
1 Pet. 5:12		X						

Bible Reference	Church(es)	Brother(s)	Saints	Believer(s)	Body	Temple	Disciple(s)	Household
Heb. 2:11		X						
Heb. 2:12a		X						
Heb. 2:12b	X							
Heb. 2:17		X						
Heb. 3:1		X						
Heb. 3:6								X
Heb. 3:12		X						
Heb. 6:10			X					
Heb. 10:19		X						
Heb. 10:21								X
Heb. 13:22		X						
Heb. 13:23		X						
Heb. 13:24			X					
2 Pet. 1:10		X						
2 Pet. 3:15		X						
1 John 2:7		X						
1 John 2:9		X						
1 John 2:10		X						
1 John 2:11		X						
1 John 3:10		X						
1 John 3:13		X						
1 John 3:14a		X						
1 John 3:14b		X						
1 John 3:15		X						
1 John 3:16		X						
1 John 3:17		X						
1 John 4:20a		X						
1 John 4:20b		X						
1 John 4:21		X						

Bible Reference	Church(es)	Brother(s)	Saints	Believer(s)	Body	Temple	Disciple(s)	Household
1 John 5:16		X						
3 John 3		X						
3 John 5		X						
3 John 6	X							
3 John 9	X							
3 John 10a	X							
3 John 10b		X						
Jude 3			X					
Rev. 1:4	X							
Rev. 1:9		X						
Rev. 1:11	X							
Rev. 1:20a	X							
Rev. 1:20b	X							
Rev. 2:1	X							
Rev. 2:7	X							
Rev. 2:8	X							
Rev. 2:11	X							
Rev. 2:12	X							
Rev. 2:17	X							
Rev. 2:18	X							
Rev. 2:23	X							
Rev. 2:29	X							
Rev. 3:1	X							
Rev. 3:6	X							
Rev. 3:7	X							
Rev. 3:13	X							
Rev. 3:14	X							
Rev. 3:22	X							
Rev. 19:8			X					

Bible Reference	Church(es)	Brother(s)	Saints	Believer(s)	Body	Temple	Disciple(s)	Household
Rev. 22:16	X							

APPENDIX C

PAUL'S JOURNEYS—A TIME LINE

A Chronological Perspective on the New Testament Letters, Particularly as They Relate to Paul's Missionary Journeys Recorded in the Book of Acts.

PART I	PART II	PART III	PART IV
First Journey	**Second Journey**	**Third Journey & Roman Imprisonment**	**Beyond the Book of Acts**
Acts 13:1-15;35	Acts 15:36-18:22	Acts 18:23-28:31	1 Timothy (A.D. 63) Titus (A.D. 65) 2 Timothy (A.D. 66)
Galatians (A.D. 49-55)	1 Thessalonians (A.D. 51) 2 Thessalonians (A.D. 51) 1 Corinthians (A.D. 56) 2 Corinthians (A.D. 57)	Romans (A.D. 58) Philemon (A.D. 61) Ephesians (A.D. 61) Colossians (A.D. 61) Philippians (A.D. 61)	

Here are the other significant letters in the New Testament that also help us measure our churches. They are listed chronologically in the order they were written.

James (A.D. 45-50) **1 Peter (A.D. 63)** **Hebrews (A.D. 64-68)** **2 Peter (A.D. 66)**

Jude (A.D. 70-80) **1,2,3 John (A.D. 90)** **Revelation (A.D. 90s)**

Appendix D

Chronology of Paul's Life

These dates and Paul's age are approximate and may vary by several years. However, to simplify remembering these statistics, the years are arranged to coincide with the first year following Christ's birth, and, even though Christ was probably born several years before A.D. 1, I have used our current calendar. Therefore, this chart only provides a general frame of reference.

Scripture	Event	Approx. Dates*	Approx. Years*	Age
Acts 22:3	Birth and Early Years in Tarsus	A.D. 1-13	13	13
Acts 22:3; Gal. 1:14	Studies in Jerusalem under Gamaliel	A.D. 14-19	6	19
Biblical Logic and Inference	Return to Tarsus as a Tentmaker and Rabbi	A.D. 20-33	13	32
Acts 8:1; 9:1-19; Gal. 1:13	Persecution of Christians and Conversion	A.D. 33-34	1	33
Gal. 1:15-17	Stay in Arabia	A.D. 34-36	3	36
Gal. 1:17; Acts 9:19-22	Return to Damascus	A.D. 37	Several months	37

Scripture	Event	Approx. Dates*	Approx. Years*	Age
Acts 9:26; Gal. 1:18	Return to Jerusalem	A.D. 38	Several months	38
Acts 9:30	Return to Tarsus	A.D. 38-44	6	44
Acts 11:25-26	Joins Barnabas in Antioch	A.D. 45	1	45
Acts 13:1—14:28	First Missionary Journey	A.D. 46-48	3	48
Acts 15:1-35	Council of Jerusalem	A.D. 49	Several months	49
Acts 15:36—18:22	Second Missionary Journey	A.D. 49-52	3	52
Acts 18:23—21:16	Third Missionary Journey	A.D. 53-58	6	58
Acts 21:17—23:30	Arrest in Jerusalem	A.D. 58	Several months	58
Acts 25:31—26:32	Confinement in Caesarea	A.D. 58-60	2	60
Acts 27:1—28:16	Trip to Rome	A.D. 60-61	1	61
Acts 28:17-31	First Imprisonment in Rome	A.D. 61-63	2	63
Pastoral Epistles	Continued Ministry	A.D. 63-66	3	66
	Martyrdom	A.D. 67	Several months	67

*Note: I developed this particular time line when writing the book *Paul: Living for the Call of Christ* (Nashville, TN: Broadman and Holman Publishers, 2000), p. 6.